P9-CNI-101

About the Author

Paul H. Schneiter is a 16-year veteran of "fund-raising wars," on "fronts" ranging from hospitals and universities to symphony orchestras, a chapter of the Red Cross, and a cross section of other nonprofit institutions. In his present position as Manager of Marketing for LDS Foundation, he helps to develop philanthropic support for the worldwide educational and religious programs of the Mormon Church, including Brigham Young University, Ricks College, and Church-owned and -operated elementary schools throughout Polynesia. He is a graduate, *cum laude,* of Utah State University (journalism), and has done graduate work at the University of Utah and Brigham Young University. He is the winner of over 30 national awards for excellence in fund-raising communication (print and electronic media) from half-a-dozen organizations, and is co-author (with Donald T. Nelson) of "The 13 Most Common Fund-Raising Mistakes and How to Avoid Them."

The Art of ASKING

How to Solicit Philanthropic Gifts

Paul H. Schneiter

Second Edition

FUND-RAISING INSTITUTE

For Pat

Library of Congress Catalog Card Number: 77-78993

Copyright © 1985 by Fund-Raising Institute, Box 365, Ambler, Pa. 19002-0365, USA.

Printed in the United States of America. No part of this publication may be reproduced, stored in a retrieval system, or transmitted in any form or by any means — electronic, mechanical, photocopying, recording, or otherwise — without the prior written permission of the publisher. FRI is a registered trademark of Balthaser North American Corporation, Inc. First edition published in 1978 as "The Art of Asking: A Handbook for Successful Fund Raising" by Walker and Company, Inc., and published simultaneously in Canada by Beaverbooks, Limited. First edition copyrighted © 1978 by Paul H. Schneiter.

ISBN 0-930807-00-6

CONTENTS

FOREWORD

Fund raising is an intriguing art. It demands mastery of an odd assortment of skills, some of which seem altogether incompatible. The successful fund raiser must be both gentle and aggressive, modest and proud, quiet and outspoken. In recent years fund raising has been further complicated by dramatic changes in both technology and taxation.

Nevertheless, American fund raising is thriving as never before. Fund raisers, amateur and professional, are at the very center of some of the most significant events in American community and national life. They are also at the center of an enormous financial enterprise. If you count contributions of money and of labor in the form of volunteer work, the dollar value of American philanthropy is measured in billions of dollars each year. The amount Americans give has increased steadily since 1910. Outlook for the decade ahead? More of the same.

Millions of Americans are directly involved in fund-raising management and solicitation. Relatively few of these, however, are seasoned veterans. Some are simply doing their civic duty, such as the auto dealer who agrees to head up the United Way campaign in his town. Some are former athletes and coaches, insurance agents, and real estate men hired as development officers by junior colleges or relatively small hospitals. Some are teachers who have taken on an additional assignment. Some are active members of their faith who have heeded the call of their religious leaders. Some are housewives doing their part for PTA and Little League. And some are very young, such as the Girl Scouts who sell cookies door to door.

Many, frankly, are scared. And they have a right to be: In almost no other endeavor is one's performance so visible and measurable. Most are woefully unprepared for their fund-raising roles. Selling automobiles or insurance is one thing, but asking people to give their money to a cause, institution, or program is quite another.

And make no mistake: Asking *is* the heart of the matter. You *must* ask if you hope to receive. Furthermore, many people not only expect you to ask, they actually look forward to it. According to Dr. Ernest Dichter, nationally recognized motivational psychologist, being asked helps to satisfy the human need to be wanted, to be courted, to play God.

How do people learn the art of asking? Do they study it in college? No — most colleges don't teach it. Do they learn it from friends or business associates? Not really. Do they master it in three-day seminars in Las Vegas? They try. Do they learn it by trial and error? Probably. And the results are usually disappointing, if not disastrous. At best they waste too much time, talent, and material. At worst, they tarnish otherwise respectable careers as well as the name of the cause for which they seek funds.

The purpose of this book is to help people learn the art of asking. It is a comprehensive, practical, no-nonsense guide to fund raising (it does not, however, cover governmental grantmaking). It is short on theory and long on practice. It is suitable for both individual and institutional use. Although it was written expressly for those in the range of zero to moderate fund-raising experience, veteran fund raisers will find that it offers provocative new perspectives and insights.

This book is based on my many years of experience with a large, diversified organization that has successfully raised millions of dollars for many different kinds of institutions. Included among these are the largest church-owned university and junior college in America. Although my experience has touched all aspects of fund raising, my specialty has been fund-raising communication. That circumstance accounts for the title of the book as well as for its special emphasis on the tools and techniques of asking.

My hope is that the book will help those whose causes are just.

Paul H. Schneiter

ACKNOWLEDGMENTS

The author gratefully acknowledges the assistance of his colleagues and friends in LDS Foundation whose knowledge, experience, and willingness to help made this book possible. Special thanks are expressed to Donald T. Nelson, Barry B. Preator, and Sandra Barrus, as well as to William F. Balthaser of the Fund-Raising Institute.

In addition, the author wishes to recognize the thoughtful and valuable contributions of the following individuals: Nanette Atlas, Ralph E. Chamberlain, Ellen G. Estes, Robert M. Holcombe, Mark J. Howard, Neal H. Hurwitz, Charles E. Lawson, William C. McGinly, Brian O'Connell, Helen O'Rourke, Alan R. Robinson, Merrill R. Petty, Howard M. Schwartz, Conrad Squires, Alden B. Tueller, Byron Welch, Stephen Wertheimer, and J. Richard Wilson. Also, American Association of Fund-Raising Counsel, Inc.; American Cancer Society, Inc.; Boys' Club of Utah County; Brigham Young University; Council for the Advancement and Support of Education; LDS Foundation; National Charities Information Bureau, Inc.; Philanthropic Advisory Service (a division of the Council of Better Business Bureaus, Inc.); Ricks College; The Foundation Center; and Weber State College.

The following figures are reproduced by permission of LDS Foundation, Provo, Utah: 4-4, 4-5, 4-11, 4-12, 4-14, 4-16, 4-18, 4-20, 6-1, 6-2, 6-3, 6-4, 6-7, 6-8. Figure 4-10 is reproduced by permission of Weber State College, Ogden, Utah. Figure 4-21 is reproduced by permission of Utah Valley Regional Medical Center, Provo, Utah. Figure 5-1 is reproduced by permission of the Boys' Club of Utah County.

WHO GIVES— AND TO WHOM?

Americans are the most generous people on earth, and American philanthropy is the envy of the world.

Sound familiar? Chances are it does — or at least some variation of it. And unlike some cherished American ideas that have fallen on hard times, this one, it's good to know, has not: Americans *are* the most generous people on earth, and American philanthropy *is* the envy of the world.

Proof? A while back, the American Association of Fund-Raising Counsel calculated that, during one specific year, Americans gave an average of $80 million per day to philanthropic causes. *Per day!* But as it turned out, that specific year wasn't even very spectacular; the nation has long since passed the $80-million-per-day figure. And money isn't all that people give. About a quarter of the American population also give their time as volunteer workers for the nonprofit causes in which they believe.

In short, while philanthropy has Greek roots (literally "loving mankind"), it has flourished and flowered in *American* soil. Americans are its preeminent practitioners, both as givers and receivers.

This chapter sets the American philanthropic scene for you. The purpose here is to help you to understand the unique drama of which you are a part, and to prepare yourself for your important role in it. Specifically, the information herein will help you to evaluate the giving patterns of individuals, foundations, and corporations (the three sources of United States philanthropic support), and to relate them to your cause. The major ways in which individuals give, from simple cash gifts to life-income agreements, are presented. And a financial summary of philanthropic giving activity in the United States for a recent decade is shown at the end of this chapter.

WHO GIVES

Who donates the billions that Americans give away? Huge, skyscraper-housed foundations? Big, multinational corporations? Actually, foundations and corporations account for only a small percentage of the sum.

Individuals. The real givers — the big charitable spenders — are *individuals.* Between 80 to 90 percent of all philanthropic dollars come from living individuals — people "just like you and me." Individuals have historically set the pace, even if you go back a few decades. In 1961, for example, individuals gave $7.5 billion versus about $1.25 billion given by foundations and corporations; in 1965 the figures were about $10 billion versus $1.80 billion. Moreover, individuals tend to give while they are alive rather than by bequest: In 1976, $23.58 billion was given by living donors and only $2.36 billion by deceased donors through bequest. Seven years later — in 1983 — the ratio remained about the same: $53.85 billion was given by living donors, and $4.52 by deceased donors. Americans apparently agree with the 18th century English religious writer L. M. Stretch who said: "Defer not charities till death. He that does so is rather liberal of another man's substance than his own."

Individuals contribute most of the money received by American religious organizations, and they contribute about half of everything received by colleges and universities.

Other facts you should know about individual giving:

- 86% of all Americans contribute to one or more charitable organizations.

- Giving correlates to income: Those who make more, give more.

- Giving also correlates to education and occupation: College graduates give two-and-a-half times more than do individuals with less than a high school diploma, and contributions by business and professional workers are nearly double those of unskilled laborers.

- Income tax itemizers give about two-and-a-half times as much as non-itemizers.

- People are most supportive of those charities that offer specific, help-oriented services, and they are most hesitant about those that provide strictly educational or information services.

- Most individuals who have made large gifts indicate that their feelings about the institution to which they gave were very important in deciding the size of their contribution.

- Contributions of lower- and middle-income taxpayers are very responsive to income and unresponsive to the after-tax cost of giving. At very high income levels, however, contributions are equally responsive to donor income and to the after-tax cost of giving.

Private foundations. The giving priorities and interests of private foundations — as well as the amount they give as a percentage of total United States philanthropy — have remained uncannily constant over the years. Even as far back as 1921, private foundations were giving most heavily to welfare, health, and education, and least to religion. Support for cultural activities, science, and social science has traditionally occupied the middle ground. Although foundation giving accounted for 9.3 percent of all giving in 1970, it accounted for only 6 percent in 1976, and fluctuated between 4.9 percent and 5.7 percent in the seven years that followed. Although there are about 22,000 active grantmaking foundations in the United States, only about 70 of these have assets of $100 million or more, and these larger foundations account for nearly one-third of the total dollar value of grants awarded annually. Because many foundations tend to give only in areas in which they are located, it is important to know that over half of all foundations are concentrated in seven states — California, Illinois, Michigan, New York, Ohio, Pennsylvania, and Texas. It is also important for you to know that company-sponsored foundations are experiencing rapid growth: Between 1975 and 1981, for example, they increased by 51 percent.

Corporations. In the early and mid-1970's, corporations were less than promising sources of philanthropic support for charities in the United States. In 1973, for example, corporations accounted for only 3.9 percent of all giving. In recent years, however, that has changed — a result, in part, of moves toward "corporate citizenship" and "enlightened corporate social consciousness." In fact, in 1981 corporations overtook foundations in giving ($3 billion versus $2.62 billion). Although corporations' share of total United States giving may shift somewhat over the years, it is unlikely — barring some economic catastrophe — that they will ever again be a distant third in philanthropic support. It should be recognized, too, that corporations support charitable causes with more than direct financial aid — they give their time, products, and services as well.

Corporations tend to give the most to education, followed by health and human services, culture and art, civic and community activities, and "other" (religious causes, women's activities, and international relief).

Fund raisers should understand that corporations exist primarily to make a profit — not to give away their stockholders' money. Consequently, corporate philanthropy is strongly influenced by hard-nosed business decisions, and probably always will be.

WHO RECEIVES

Of the major targets of American philanthropy, religion always leads the dollar totals by a huge margin, followed by education, and health and hospitals. (These two categories receive almost identical percentages of support year in and year out.) Social services, arts and humanities, civic and public, and "other" follow, in that order.

> *For where your treasure is,*
> *there will your heart be also.*
> —MATTHEW 6:21

Religion. Religious organizations receive from 40 to 50 percent of all funds contributed. Keep in mind that many contributions to religious organizations are used in some down-to-earth ways.

In fact, about one-fifth goes for nonsacramental purposes. Religious groups operate schools, hospitals, social welfare agencies, feed-the-hungry programs, shelters, etc.

Because church membership and attendance have been declining in recent years for some denominations, and because giving to religion usually takes place at church services, some religious leaders have expressed concern about the outlook for philanthropic support of churches in the years ahead. Those concerns should be weighed, however, against the fact that other denominations are experiencing substantial *increases* in membership and attendance — and in philanthropic support. Consequently, there is good reason to believe that religion will continue to occupy its preeminent position as the leading recipient of philanthropic support in America.

Education. Historically, higher education has received over half of all contributions to education, with the balance earmarked for elementary and secondary schools, independent institutions (military and boarding schools, for example), and a variety of other institutions. Many of these are church-related. Corporations have steadily increased their support of higher education, and today they account for over 20 percent of the total philanthropic support received by the nation's colleges and universities. There is evidence to suggest that increases in the number of institutions that are organizing fund-raising activities accounts, in part, for the increase in corporate support of higher education. Another factor is the growth in corporate-sponsored matching gift programs.

Health and hospitals. Of the billions given annually for health purposes, most is earmarked for the following: personal health care; local, regional, and national health agencies, to be used in a variety of ways; endowing health institutions; and constructing and equipping health facilities. Smaller amounts go to medical research and to the United Way and Red Cross to meet many different health needs. For many years, the American Cancer Society and the American Heart Association have attracted the most philanthropic support among national health agencies. Many observers feel that cost-containment moves by hospitals, the growth of for-profit hospitals, and changes in the part the federal government plays in health care are certain to have spillover effects — some good and some bad — on fund-raising efforts in behalf of health and hospitals.

Social services. Social service agencies are concerned with improving the quality of many different aspects of American community life. Among these agencies are the Boy Scouts of America, Girl Scouts of America, Boys' Clubs of America, Salvation Army, USO, Urban League, Travelers Aid, American Red Cross, and YMCA/YWCA. Unquestionably, the United Way is the dominant force in raising funds for such agencies. But the United Way does more than raise money: It helps to rally support for social services from many different community elements. The United Way also works with member agencies and community leaders to plan for optimum use of all contributed funds. In the early 1980's, United Way turned its attention to a growing national problem: the homeless and malnourished. The Combined Federal Campaign, which concentrates its efforts on federal government workers, is proving to be a helpful adjunct to the work of United Way, as are "alternative funds" and Black United Funds.

Arts and humanities. This category includes programs in dance, literature, art, museums, music, theatre, public broadcasting, and folk art — to name a few. Most of the support for these programs comes, and will probably continue to come, from the traditional sources — individuals, corporations, and foundations, and from earned income (such as ticket sales). One might suppose that support for the arts and humanities would be somewhat volatile, on the ground that donors might be susceptible to being redirected to other, more pressing causes (hunger, homelessness, child abuse, etc.). The fact is, however, that the philanthropic support received by the arts and humanities as a percentage of total United States giving has remained remarkably constant over the years — right around 6 percent.

Civic and public. Urban development, equal rights, legal services, environmental causes, and economic development are among the recipients in this category. Perhaps because they perceive them as noncontroversial and rich in public relations potential, corporations tend to respond warmly to certain, sharply defined civic and public affairs projects. Two cases in point: the 1984 Olympiad in Los Angeles and the restoration of the Statue of Liberty. Corporate support for these projects was both generous and enthusiastic.

Is it possible for an agency to be *too* successful in stating its case for philanthropic support? Perhaps. Consider this fact: With the passage of federal and state laws to clean up the environment, support for agencies that have sought enactment of those very laws has waned. Donors seem to be saying to themselves, in effect, "That problem is under control. It's time to move on to other, still-to-be-solved problems."

Other. This category consists of a mix of organizations that are involved in foreign aid and relief, technical and educational assistance, and foundation endowment. World crises directly affect the level of funding received by agencies in this category; i.e., the 1980 earthquake in Southern Italy that killed 4,800 people and the 1984 Ethiopian famine in which tens of thousands of Africans lost their lives.

HOW CONTRIBUTIONS ARE MADE

The "how" of corporate and foundation giving can be quickly covered. Corporations give in cash, services and materials — but mostly in cash. Foundations give cash almost exclusively.

In contrast, individuals give in many different ways, all of which are influenced by federal and state tax laws. Individual giving can be divided into two broad categories: gifts made during life and gifts by will (upon death). The information that follows is designed only to *introduce* you to *some* of the mechanics of individual giving. The intent is to give you an awareness-level understanding of the major ways in which people give. Complete details, impact of state laws, qualifying statements and footnotes (of which there are many), new Internal Revenue Service rulings, and other important data are not included. They are well beyond the scope of this section, and they are much more complex than the following descriptions would suggest. Also, the giving methods described in this book are based on the laws and customs of the United States; readers in other nations will have different laws and customs to contend with. *Consequently, it is extremely important that you seek legal counsel when you address these matters and relate them to real-life prospects and gifts.*

Outright gifts of money. Most individual giving takes this form. It is direct and uncomplicated. It typically involves dropping a quarter into a supermarket charity canister, or a $5 bill onto the church collection plate, or a check into the mail to one's alma mater. Increasingly, such giving is being done automatically — by payroll deduction to United Way, for example.

A donor who gives cash to qualifying organizations (schools, hospitals, churches, and other publicly supported charities) can deduct the gift on his or her federal income tax return. The donor can claim deductions for such gifts up to a certain percent of his or her adjusted gross income. If he or she gives over that ceiling, the donor can deduct the excess for the next several years, or until it is used up. Donors who make cash contributions receive another benefit: They can reduce their estates, and, therefore, their estate taxes.

Appreciated securities and real estate. If the contributed property (stock, house, farm, etc.) has been held for more than a certain length of time, the donor receives two important tax benefits: 1) a charitable deduction for the present fair market value of the gift, and 2) avoidance of capital gains tax payable on the appreciation in value if he or she had sold the property.

Appreciated art works, other personal property. Paintings, coin collections, books, and other tangible property are commonly given to charitable organizations. If the property's use relates directly to the receiving charity's function (such as a painting given to a publicly supported art museum), the donor can deduct the item's full fair market value and not be subject to capital gains tax on the appreciation. If the property does not relate to the charity's exempt function, the donor must deduct less.

Life insurance. Gifts of life insurance typically take the following form: Mr. Jones decides he has more life insurance than he needs. Rather than cancel one of his policies, he gives it to his church. He also gives his church an amount equal to the annual premium on the policy. On his federal income tax return, Mr. Jones can deduct the current fair market value of the policy plus the amount he gives annually to pay the premium.

Life income agreements (planned gifts). These are growing in popularity because they make it possible for individuals to: give to charity immediately, receive a lifetime income, and receive substantial tax benefits. There are several types of life income agreements and many variations of each type. Five of the most common are: annuity trust, unitrust, gift annuity, deferred payment gift annuity, and pooled income fund. Some require fairly large gifts; others can be made by giving only a few thousand dollars.

Gifts by will. In a typical gift by will (bequest), the donor bequeaths a stated sum or an interest in an estate to a charitable cause. If the total estate is the right size, the estate tax will be reduced, making the estate's actual "cost" for the gift lower than the amount received by the charity.

But the typical way isn't the only way to make a charitable bequest. There are variations. For example, the donor can leave his or her estate in a charitable annuity trust. An heir can be designated to receive a fixed annual income from that trust for life. But when the heir dies, the trust ends and the principal goes to the charity.

Or, another variation: A donor leaves his or her entire estate to the spouse, but in the form of two trusts. When the spouse dies, the principal of one of the trusts is distributed as the spouse's will directs. But the principal of the other trust goes to a charity specified by the original donor.

These and other variations allow donors to reduce the impact of taxation on their estates, thus maximizing the amount of the estate that's available for the family and for favorite charities. These are rather standard forms of estate planning, but they are also sophisticated forms. To decide on the right form, and to plan a donor's estate to take advantage of it, is work for highly trained specialists — lawyers, accountants, development officers, trust officers, etc.

PHILANTHROPY IN AMERICA FOR THE DECADE 1974-1983

Total Contributions: $426.20 Billion

Givers (billions of $)

Individuals: $350.64 (82.27 percent of total)

Bequests: $ 29.93 (7.02 percent of total)

Foundations: $ 24.29 (5.70 percent of total)

Corporations: $ 21.34 (5.01 percent of total)

Receivers (billions of $)

Religion: $196.54 (46.11 percent of total)

Health &
Hospitals: $ 59.85 (14.04 percent of total)

Education: $ 59.35 (13.93 percent of total)

Social
Services: $ 42.59 (9.99 percent of total)

Arts &
Humanities: $ 28.05 (6.51 percent of total)

Civic &
Public: $ 12.34 (2.94 percent of total)

Other: $ 27.48 (6.45 percent of total)

Source: "Giving USA" annual reports issued by the
American Association of Fund-Raising Counsel, Inc.

2 ▦ FRI
MAKING THE MOST OF THE HUMAN NEED TO GIVE

To succeed in fund raising, you must acquire a working knowledge of the forces that motivate people to give. Be forewarned, however: Even in acts of charity, selflessness does not rule the day. The fact is, human beings give their wealth to other human beings for eight basic reasons or combinations thereof, all of which are at least in part self-fulfilling. This is a practical, not a cynical, assessment.

Religious beliefs. Some individuals make gifts because the teachings of their religion direct them to do so, and because they seek the spiritual and temporal rewards promised to the obedient. Biblical injunctions to give to the poor and needy abound in the Old and New Testaments. In his instructions to Moses on Mount Sinai, the Lord tells his people to relieve a brother "fallen in decay" and to "Take thou no usury of him..." (Leviticus 25:35, 36). Amos and Micah issue a clear call for justice for the poor. And Moses commands the Israelites to "open thine hand wide unto thy brother, to thy poor, and to thy needy..." (Deuteronomy 15:11).

The story of the Good Samaritan is representative of New Testament teachings about charity. You will recall that a certain man traveling from Jerusalem to Jericho "fell among thieves" (Luke 10:30) and was, in effect, mugged and left to die. A priest and a Levite passed him by, but a "certain Samaritan...had compassion on him, bound up his wounds...set him on his own beast, and brought him to an inn, and took care of him" (Luke 10:33, 34). Unquestionably, those are charitable acts, but the Samaritan goes further: "And on the morrow when he departed, he took out two pence, and gave them to the host [innkeeper], and said unto him, Take care of him: and whatsoever thou spendest more, when I come again, I will repay thee" (Luke 10:35).

Paul says that every man should give ungrudgingly, "for God loveth a cheerful giver" (2 Corinthians, 9:7). Paul also tells his followers to labor with their hands so that they can "give to him that needeth" (Ephesians 4:28).

Other great religious movements, especially those of the East, repeatedly implore help for the poor and needy. Buddhism, for example, stresses compassion for suffering; Islam, the responsibility of the wealthy to the disadvantaged.

Guilt. There can be little doubt that feelings of guilt — justified or unjustified — are factors in a significant number of philanthropic gifts. This is especially true in modern America, where the plight of the underprivileged has received comprehensive public exposure. Through the searching eye of television, millions of Americans have been made painfully aware of Appalachian poverty, migrant worker malnutrition, and the horrors of Negro slavery. In fact, some sociologists now speak routinely of "mass guilt complexes."

It is also reasonably safe to assume that the larger the gift, the greater the likelihood that guilt feelings motivated it. Why? Because in a society of haves and have-nots, the accumulation of great wealth — whether inherited, honestly earned, or stolen — inevitably gives rise to feelings of guilt. It pressed on this point, donors will deny it. This response is understandable, not merely because it is a common defensive reaction, but also because guilt feelings often go unrecognized by the individuals who harbor them. When people give their money to charity, they have reason to believe that they are benefiting society. That knowledge helps to relieve their guilt feelings.[1]

Guilt as a motivating factor in giving is directly in evidence in the "conscience funds" maintained by many police forces. Individuals can anonymously make restitution for unpunished wrongs through such funds. A common pattern is for middle-aged people to send in checks to pay for crimes committed in their youth.[2]

Reputable fund raisers recognize the role guilt plays in giving but they are circumspect about using it. They know that exploiting a prospective donor's guilt feelings will not build mutual trust and respect. They also know that such tactics are not conducive to a successful long-term cultivation and fund-raising program in the community of which they are a part.

Recognition. Man longs for immortality. The giving of gifts to which one's name is attached is one way to achieve at least a degree of immortality. One Greek donor of long ago was refreshingly candid on this subject. He requested that his gift be reported on at least three marble tablets: "...so that to citizens and non-citizens alike...my philanthropic and kindly act may be evident and well known...my idea is to achieve immortality in making such a just and kindly disposal."[3]

The list of Americans who have followed the Greek's example is long and well known. Their names also appear on marble tablets — attached to buildings: Stanford University, Carnegie Free Public Library, Whitney Museum, Wrigley Field. The list goes on.

The names of other donors who wanted to be remembered are associated with important prizes (Pulitzer, Nobel); with scholarships and fellowships (Rhodes, Danforth); and with thousands of programs, institutes, swimming pools, centers, clinics, museums, parks, laboratories, art galleries, hospitals — you name it — across the country.

While no conclusive research has been done on the subject, the number of donors who give anonymously — and thus clearly signal that they do not want recognition — is probably fewer than 10 in 100. At least some of those who give anonymously do so not for reasons of modesty, but to avoid the public exposure that could send flocks of fund raisers to their doorsteps.

You must openly and honestly recognize the ego needs of prospective donors — and, where practical, accommodate them. If individuals, as a condition of making gifts, want their names attached to them, that is their right. All such gifts, however, should be approved by the president or governing board of the receiving institution before commitments of any kind are made to donors. In some circumstances, institutions would clearly compromise their principles by accepting the money and names of certain donors — for example, persons who are known to be inimical to the recipient's ethics and goals.

Every institution would do well to delineate clearly its policy on naming buildings, rooms, programs, etc. Among the questions to be resolved is this one: What percentage of the total cost of a building (or room or program) must a donor contribute in order for it to be named after him or her? The figure arrived at is less important than is establishing a written policy on the matter. Obviously, though, no building, room, or program should be "sold" to a donor for anything less than a "controlling interest" in it — 51 percent or more.

Because of the importance of recognition to many donors, always ask them if they want publicity. Even if they say no, they will appreciate your thoughtfulness in raising the question. If they say yes, you should work closely with your institution's public relations office or news bureau, or directly with the local press to see that the donors' desires are met. And here's a helpful followup suggestion: Send donors press clippings with a cover letter thanking them for their contribution.

In most cases it is in your interest to give donors public recognition. Such publicity not only draws favorable attention to your cause, but it also applies social pressure on others to contribute — particularly the wealthy. Most of us have watched television fund-raising marathons in which, say, Bill Stubbs, a bowler in the All-City League, calls in with a $20 pledge and challenges all other bowlers to match it. Bill is applying social pressure. But the fact is, the technique is effective with big donors, too. When you publicize the $100,000 gift of Mr. Blank, Elmville's well-known real estate developer, you and Mr. Blank in effect challenge others in Mr. Blank's income bracket to give a comparable gift. In short, the desire to keep up with the Joneses is a philanthropic fact of life, and publicity is an excellent way for you to capitalize on it.

Self-preservation and fear. Some people give to charity in an effort to save themselves — from hell, from disease, from militant minority groups — from anything that they believe threatens their survival.

Fear of hell comes through with unforgettable force in the opening lines of a will cited by Courtney Kenney, an English critic of charities: "For the benefit of my poor soul, God help me, as a kind of atonement for the great crimes I have committed against the commandments of God, I do award...."[4]

National health campaigns capitalize on Americans' fear of certain diseases — and on the promise of cures. Do any of these sound familiar? "We're Fighting For Your Life" — "Money Walks: Give to Easter Seals" — "Conquer Cancer with a Check and a Checkup" — "A Massive, Unprecedented Human Tragedy Is In the Making" — "Diabetes: To Most It's Just a Word; to Some It's a Way of Life."

If you doubt that health fund raisers play on peoples' fears, consider this fact: Year in and year out, the American Cancer Society raises substantially more than the American Heart Association, despite the fact that heart disease claims about three times as many lives as cancer. Logically, fighting heart disease should have greater philanthropic appeal than fighting cancer. However, people *perceive* cancer as the greater threat — a fact confirmed by surveys that show cancer is the disease Americans fear above all others.

It is a common practice for whites who live in cities beset with racial tensions to contribute to minority causes. While some of these donors are responding sincerely to an awakened awareness of the plight of minorities, others are simply buying protection — for their lives and property.

When war broke out between Egypt and Israel, the American Jewish community responded with a remarkable outpouring of aid funds for their homeland. At a meeting in the Waldorf-Astoria Hotel on the day fighting began, New York Jews pledged $1 million a minute during one quarter-hour period. And within the week, Jews nationwide had given $90 million. Many of the donors redeemed life insurance policies, went into debt, and sold their cars.[5] Self-preservation — in its broadest and noblest sense — is very much in evidence in this fund-raising accomplishment.

Tax rewards. Many Americans believe that philanthropic giving is motivated above all else by tax considerations. Unquestionably, the United States Internal Revenue Code offers special tax deductions, exclusions, and exemptions to those who give. Under these circumstances, gifts — especially when given by the very wealthy — cost donors only a fraction of their face value.

Nevertheless, it is not safe to assume that taxes are a major consideration in giving. According to a University of Michigan survey, only at the $100,000-plus level do more than 50 percent of donors cite taxes as a major factor. Only one taxpayer in five knows, even roughly, how much in taxes each added dollar of deductions will save. And only 12 times in thousands of interviews did people offer tax reasons for changing their giving.[6] The Fund-Raising Institute finds that donors rate tax considerations as 10th or later in priority,[7] and in a comprehensive study of major donors' motivations in giving, consultant Jerold Panas found that tax incentives were often the *least* important consideration.[8] Finally, in a survey of over 200 major donors, the American Association of Fund-Raising Counsel found that only 11.5 percent rated tax benefits as very important.[9]

Bear in mind, too, that philanthropic giving thrived long before income tax laws. For example, Rockefeller, Carnegie, and Stanford made huge gifts with no tax incentives whatsoever.[10] And today many organizations receive substantial contributions, even though they are not "IRS qualified." This means, of course, that those who support them cannot claim their contributions as charitable income tax deductions.

When you offer prospective donors tax deductions as an incentive for giving, you offer them nothing unique: Thousands of other tax-exempt institutions offer precisely the same thing. The moral here is do not oversell tax angles; rather, sell the worthiness of your institution to receive a contribution and its ability to use it with maximum effectiveness. The time to talk about tax rewards is *after* your prospect is sold on your institution or project. This strategy is important for another reason: It enables prospects to maintain their integrity. They don't want to come across to you as people whose overriding interest is saving taxes.

Obligation. We have all seen headlines like these: "Immigrant Gives Priceless Paintings to White House" — "Grateful Patient Leaves Fortune to Hospital" — "Harvard Grad Establishes Endowed Chair" — "Oil Tycoon Bequeaths Estate to Secretary."

These donors are giving, at least in part, out of a sense of obligation or a feeling of indebtedness. Their quoted statements invariably read like this: "I wanted to do something to pay back my alma mater for all that it did for me," or "I'm alive today because of Midtown Hospital and its doctors and nurses."

In some cases, donors who give out of a sense of obligation are also giving to achieve recognition. The former simply provides a socially acceptable "cover" for the latter.

Obligation as a fund-raising technique has been used most frequently — and infamously — in direct mail campaigns. Remember the Ident-o-tag? It was the miniature license plate for key chains sent out in the millions by the Disabled American Veterans. You didn't ask for it. It simply arrived, uninvited, each year in your mail box. The Ident-o-tag strategy was to make the recipient feel obligated to contribute. It worked: In one year, the Ident-o-tag raised nearly $21 million for the DAV!"

For sheer bad taste, however, the Ident-o-tag must move over for a technique once widely employed by a religious sect. Their *modus operandi* involved stationing college-age women in airports serving large cities. The women would rush up to travelers — males made the best targets — and pin a carnation on them, then gush something like, "A handsome carnation for a handsome man." With the carnation — and the compliment — firmly secured, an appeal for funds followed. It invariably succeeded.

The most important thing to remember about obligation as a factor in giving is that it must originate naturally with the prospective donor. You cannot create it, and you should not try.

Pride and self-respect. Every healthy and mature personality wants to be well thought of by others...wants to be perceived as someone of sensitivity, selflessness, and compassion. Individuals who make philanthropic gifts can, in almost a single stroke, powerfully project this positive image to others. Insightful fund raisers understand this fact, and — as a result — they treat prospects *as they want them to become,* always assigning to them praiseworthy qualities and motives. They say, in effect: "I know you respond to the finer things in life; I know you care about young people; I know you have the maturity and wisdom to see beyond your place and time; I know you are a caring, giving person."

Prospective donors, having been thus elevated in the eyes of their beholders, are reluctant to do anything to lower themselves (i.e., saying "no" in response to a request for a charitable contribution).

Pressure. By and large, you cannot control the factors described so far in this chapter. You can turn them to your advantage if they exist naturally, but you cannot control them. Fortunately, that is not true of pressure.

Professional fund raisers may react with alarm to the author's use of the word "pressure." Some would say that it is appropriately applied to certain used-car-lot operations but not to properly established and managed philanthropic organizations. They would prefer "marketing," "salesmanship," or even "education." They may be right, and consequently it is important for you to understand that "pressure" as used here is not meant in any negative sense. It is meant, rather, in this sense: In the final analysis, the fund raiser must confront the prospect and ask for a contribution, and this act — in and of itself — constitutes "pressure."

By their very nature, personal appeals or even telephone appeals for contributions involve pressure and are extremely difficult for most people to resist. Such appeals have an especially high probability of success when they are made on a one-to-one basis by respected, well-known community or public figures. The services of a respected basketball coach, for example, in a telephone campaign to raise college athletic funds can prove invaluable. What UCLA alumnus could have turned down an appeal from Johnny Wooden at the height of his coaching career?

Social pressure to give can be downright devastating in certain situations. Can you resist, for example, adding to the church collection plate when those to your left, right, rear and front are giving — and watching? And can you resist the plea of a bright-eyed high school girl and her comely companion to buy a paper poppy in, say, downtown Philadelphia?

Some fund-raising campaigns involving kits that pass from neighbor to neighbor make exceptionally effective use of peer pressure. For example, an Easter Seal fund-raising kit featured a large, sturdy envelope with a flap on which were printed the column headings "Name," "Address," and "Amt." Recipients of the kit were instructed to deposit their contribution, fill in the information on the flap, and then "pass this kit to your neighbor right away." The instructions to volunteers in charge of circulating the kits were especially direct: "You may wish to make your own gift first. This will make it easier for others to give. Write your name, address, and amount on Line 1 on the kit flap. (Experience shows that the larger your gift, the larger will be your neighbors' gifts. Please set the pace!)"

Churches that hold "cake auctions" and similar events also make skillful use of peer pressure. One church raised over $1,000 for a new organ by inviting mothers and daughters to bake and decorate cakes for a "most original cake" contest. The cakes were then auctioned off to the highest bidders — usually fathers and grandfathers — at a well-attended church anniversary party. Paternal pride carried the day!

Although you may wish it were otherwise, pressure is essential in raising money. Just as you cannot make an omelet without breaking eggs, you cannot raise money without applying pressure. You must believe enough in your cause to ask directly, forcefully, and convincingly. You must use the most influential people available to you: the mayor of your city, director of your hospital, president of your college, leader of your church. And you must *never* apologize. True, you will probably offend someone at some point along the way. One fund-raising pro shrugs this off with the observation, "The dogs bark, but the caravan moves on." He recognizes — and you should, too — that fund raisers are bound to suffer difficulties enroute to their goals. He also recognizes, however, that those difficulties cannot stop the forward progress of fund raisers who persevere, and that — in the act of asking — they will flatter more people than they will offend, especially if they ask for handsome sums and involve attractive, popular personalities in the process.

People who sincerely believe in the correctness of their cause are pleasantly bold about asking. They honestly believe that their cause is worthy of people's financial support. But more than that, they believe that the *donors themselves* will benefit in at least two ways by giving to them: 1) They will be publicly identifying themselves with a respected, worthwhile cause — a move that will inevitably be helpful to them; and 2) they will receive great personal satisfaction — inner peace, if you will — from the knowledge that they are helping to further that cause.

This chapter has dealt with the identifiable, measurable, predictable factors that motivate acts of charity. Some of what has been said may come across as callous, and you may well ask, "But don't some people give out of goodness and decency — out of a sincere desire to help?" Yes, they do. Some people are charitable in the purest, most spiritual sense of the word. They give because they love mankind, because they are sensitive to the suffering of others, because they truly want to share what they have with those who have less. If you stay in fund raising very long, you will meet these noble people. And if you are patient and observant, they will rekindle your faith in mankind and increase your own capacity to give and love.

Notes

1. Gerald S. Soroker, "Fund-Raising for Philanthropy" (Pittsburgh: Pittsburgh Jewish Publication and Education Foundation, 1974), p. 18.
2. George C. Kirstein, "Better Giving: The New Needs of American Philanthropy" (Boston: Houghton Mifflin Company, 1975), p. 5.
3. Benedict Nightingale, "Charities" (London: Allen Lane, 1973), p. 103.
4. Ibid., p. 124.
5. Time, June 16, 1967.
6. The Wall Street Journal, June 11, 1975.
7. Tips of the Month, Fund-Raising Institute, Third Edition.
8. Jerold Panas, "Mega Gifts: Who Gives Them, Who Gets Them" (Chicago: Pluribus Press, Inc., 1984), pp. 141-151.
9. "Giving USA, 1982 Annual Report" (New York: American Association of Fund-Raising Counsel, Inc., 1982), p. 10.
10. George C. Kirstein, op. cit., p. 8.
11. Harvey Katz, "GIVE! Who Gets Your Charity Dollar?" (Garden City, New York: Anchor Press, 1974), p. 124.

BEFORE YOU ASK

Fund raising is a lot like house painting: Most of the work and some of the greatest challenges are in *preparing* to do the job, rather than in the job itself. This chapter takes you through the preparatory steps that are indispensable to effective solicitation.

ESTABLISHING THE CAUSE

Not surprisingly, America's most successful political campaigns have been keyed to causes — to well-articulated, pressing public concerns often expressed in labels or declarations: "The New Frontier"; "The Great Society"; "Let us reason together"; "We want to make America proud again"; etc. Successful fund-raising campaigns have many times taken a similar tack: "It's a matter of life and breath"; " United Way — thanks to you, it's working"; "It hurts to go to bed hungry"; "Lend a hand."

Well-conceptualized and well-communicated causes have enormous power to coalesce public opinion and to motivate people to act. The organization or institution for which you seek funds need not have a slick slogan, but it must have a believable cause — it must stand for something that people can perceive as important to them and to the things they cherish.

At least two factors make a cause believable — impact and immediacy.

Impact. Your organization must have direct impact on the lives of those whom you intend to solicit. People must be inclined to say, when they hear about your aspirations, "Yes, it's *important* that we do that." Sometimes impact is mostly a matter of geography. If you're a turkey farmer who lives 600 miles from a big airport, you aren't likely to respond to an appeal from an association of turkey farmers for funds to fight noisy jet aircraft. But what if you and your turkeys are only 50 miles from a major airport?

Immediacy. Your organization must be involved in work that merits attention *now, today, as soon as possible;* hence, "We want to cure cancer *in your lifetime."* Without a strong sense of immediacy, you will have difficulty stirring prospects and volunteers to action.

A third factor, one easily overlooked, also deserves attention. It involves *you* — your attitude, commitment, outlook — the whole way in which you view the worth of your work. You cannot function with maximum effectiveness on behalf of a cause in which you do not fully believe and to which you yourself have not made a financial contribution. If you find yourself in that position, you should, as a matter of personal integrity, step aside and give your organization a chance to strengthen its leadership.

An important part of establishing the cause is the *case statement.* This is a declaration telling what your organization does, what it has accomplished, what it intends to do in the future, and why it is worthy of people's financial support. Put the statement in *writing.* This is important for two reasons. First, it will help you to communicate with volunteers and prospects (you'll refer to it repeatedly in preparing news releases, proposals, brochures, letters, and speeches). And second, it will force you and your colleagues to give the matter the serious, thoughtful attention it deserves. Many case statements are too long (few people want to read 1,500 words all about *your* organization), too self-congratulatory, too inward-looking and provincial, too noncommittal. An example of a short but effective case statement used by the American Cancer Society is presented in Figure 3-1 at the end of this chapter.

BUILDING THE ORGANIZATION

Chances are, whether you are an amateur or professional fund raiser, your organization already exists — it doesn't have to be built. But even if that is the case, an understanding of the basics of fund-raising organization will make you a better fund raiser. It will also prepare you to expand your organization when the time comes.

Line functions in a fund-raising organization (those that contribute *directly* to raising money) typically include: planned giving, annual giving, institutional giving (foundations and corporations), and special projects (individuals and "targets of opportunity"). Staff functions (those that contribute *indirectly* to raising money) typically include: legal counsel, accounting and financial services, research, marketing, communications, and data processing/records.

In a small fund-raising organization (one to three full-time people plus volunteers), line and staff functions are, of course, combined. For example, the individual in charge of institutional giving is his or her own researcher, communicator, and accountant.

A fund-raising organization of medium size (four to nine full-time people plus volunteers) can usually afford the luxury of some separate staff functions. These should be those that require highly specialized skills, including legal counsel, data processing/records, and communications.

A fund-raising organization of large size (10 or more people plus volunteers) typically has many line and staff functions, some of which are highly specialized. Some large universities, for example, have separate "asset disposition" departments that specialize in converting non-cash donations (land, automobiles, jewelry, collections, etc.) to cash by selling them.

Model organization charts for small, medium, and large fund-raising organizations are shown in Figures 3-2, 3-3, and 3-4 at the end of this chapter.

Whether your organization consists of only you and a volunteer or two, or you and 50 others, here is a checklist that ought to be reviewed periodically. Some of your answers may suggest the need to make changes.

☐ Are your duties and those of your associates — if you have associates — about evenly divided?

☐ Are your duties and those of your associates logically, functionally grouped? For example, if you are handling planned giving, you should probably be handling special projects as well — both involve individual prospects and have many parallels.

☐ Are you making effective use of the many services available all around you? For example, if you are on a college campus, are you having the college's full-time public communications director write news releases, rather than you doing it? Are you spending time and money on image-building publications when those prepared by the college will serve just as well? Are you using student writing and art talent? (Don't overlook students as fund raisers, either. On a growing number of campuses they are proving to be extremely effective. At Brigham Young University, for example, students raised $400,000 from other students, individuals, foundations, and corporations for a new library addition.)

☐ Are you making effective use of volunteers? Some *will* perform, but only if they feel they are genuinely needed. Suggestion: Give them legitimate, challenging assignments in which the results and rewards are measurable and meaningful. (Avoid, however, imposing heavily on their time. And make certain that you recognize their service in a high-profile way, such as bestowing certificates of appreciation on them at an awards banquet.)

☐ Are you involving your secretary in planning meetings and other activities so that she has the total organizational perspective? She can handle many time-consuming details if you'll keep her fully informed.

☐ Are you preparing and maintaining a yearly calendar with key events (dates direct mail pieces are to be sent out, for example) clearly announced? Without such a calendar, you cannot efficiently plan and manage your work and that of your associates.

☐ Are you striving to grow professionally by reading current professional literature (principally magazines and newsletters), meeting and corresponding with other fund raisers (seminars, conferences, and conventions are excellent for this purpose), and affiliating with professional organizations?

☐ Are you involving professional fund-raising consultants in those inevitable instances when their services are indispensable?

☐ Are you evaluating your performance against some objective yardstick, including amount raised and operating expenses?

☐ Are you secure and mature enough to seek and to accept honest criticism, and then to take the appropriate corrective action?

☐ Are you maintaining current, detailed job descriptions for each employee position?

☐ Are you establishing *written* policies for your organization's principal functions?

☐ Are you familiar with legislation (state and federal) affecting charitable solicitation, and are you in compliance?

☐ Are you doing everything possible to maximize the amount of time you and your associates devote to *asking* (assuming you are in line positions)?

☐ Are you planning far enough ahead to be able to take your organization where you want it to be five or ten years from today?

Some thoughts about capital campaigns are appropriate here. Consultant Arthur C. Frantzreb offers this helpful definition of a capital campaign: "...usually an all-out, total constituency, person-to-person solicitation for a series of specific objectives within a given time frame with pledges or statements of intent payable over three to five years." You may someday find yourself in charge of such an all-out effort. What then? If a fund-seeking organization is involved in a capital campaign, it is usually well advised to maintain its existing organization and augment it with volunteer and part-time help only as necessary. For example, the fund raiser for a university in the Midwest met most of her staff needs for a centennial year capital campaign by using retired alumni. She asked a successful, retired industrialist to help call on corporate prospects; a retired attorney to help with planned giving presentations; and a retired physician, who had doctored the school's athletic teams for many years, to call on doctors and dentists. All served without pay.

A common practice in capital campaigns is to appoint an honorary campaign chairman and, sometimes, campaign committee. These are usually well-known, respected community, state, or even national leaders. They impart prestige, impact, and influence to the campaign. (You can usually find their names and titles in bold face type on all campaign literature!) Their main function, though, is to open doors.

Unquestionably, such individuals can be an asset. Make certain, however, that you clearly define and limit their powers and responsibilities. Make their involvement simple and easy. Tell them how long they are to serve. Don't give them a long list of assignments. Keep meetings to a minimum. Be content to use their names, influence, and contacts — this is their principal value. Finally, make them answerable to the full-time campaign director.

IDENTIFYING AND EVALUATING PROSPECTS

Consider this: Ninety percent of the money in a typical fund-raising campaign comes from 10 percent of the prospects, about 85 percent of whom are *individuals* (as opposed to foundations and corporations, which will be discussed later). This means that you must carefully identify, evaluate, and create files on *quality* individual prospects.

Where do you find prospects? Try these sources.

Past donors. Thousands of years of cumulative fund-raising experience nationwide make it clear that past donors are almost always the best prospects for future gifts. If your records have been properly maintained, you should have a file full of information about these people, including date and amount of their last gift.

Records of your organization. Categories vary, depending on the organization, but include: parents, employees, students, faculty, neighbors, friends, vendors, visitors, patients, volunteers, awardees, and individuals who in one way or another have expressed interest in your work (perhaps via a complimentary letter to you or others).

Donors to other charitable organizations. Some people make it a practice to give to charity. Giving is part of their life style. Consequently, they are excellent prospects. Watch for their names in newspaper articles, "honor rolls of giving" published by other charities, on buildings and facilities in your community, etc. Some fund raisers freely trade donor lists. This is an acceptable practice unless you have a special relationship with your donors that may preclude it. For example, a donor may have asked you to keep his contribution confidential. Obviously, giving his name to another fund raiser would be improper. Also, bear in mind that when you trade names you may alienate some donors who didn't expressly forbid the practice, but who may feel you have "used" them.

Membership rosters. These are excellent because they quickly enable you to identify people whose interests match those of your organization. For example, if you are trying to raise funds for a children's community orchestra in a city in Ohio, the membership lists of Ohio musical societies, clubs, and associations are certain to be helpful.

Telephone directory yellow pages. This one is so obvious, it's easy to overlook. Almost any fund-raising organization can find important prospects in the yellow-page listings under "A" alone, which typically includes Accountants, Architects, and Associations.

At the risk of sounding too obvious, one of the best ways to find prospects is to start looking for them! Once you begin actively to look, *many* names will come to mind.

You can, of course, *rent* a list of people who logically could be expected to have some interest in your organization. Bear in mind that if *you* can rent that list, everybody else can, too. Consequently, prospects supplied by commercial sources may well be up to their ears in fund-raising appeals from other charities.

Evaluating prospects is an extremely important function to which too many fund raisers devote too little time. Prospect evaluation usually attempts to answer three questions.

- How much can this individual give?

- Which aspect of our program is likely to interest him or her most?

- In what form is he or she most likely to give (cash, securities, trust, bequest, etc)?

Clues that will help you answer these questions include the following.

QUESTION	CLUES
How much can this individual give?	**Profession/occupation.** Is he or she a church organist or an orthodontist?
	Memberships. Does he or she golf at Provo Public or Pebble Beach?
	Hobbies. Does he or she collect string or stringed instruments?
	Possessions. Does he or she live in a house or a mansion... drive a Beetle or a Bentley...own a plot or a section?
Which aspect of our program is likely to interest him or her most?	**Source of wealth.** If he or she made it in oil, he or she *may* be interested in geology.

Special problems. If he or she has a retarded child, he or she *may* be interested in a school for exceptional children.

Need for recognition. If this need looms large in his or her life, a building bearing his or her name *may* be the only answer.

Community activities. If he's a Scouter, he *may* be interested in buying a troop bus or building a troop lodge.

Past giving patterns. If she's given to Cancer, Heart and Diabetes, she *may* also give to Cystic Fibrosis.

In what form is he or she most likely to make the gift?

Nature of the holdings. If he or she has assets that have greatly appreciated in value since they were acquired, he or she *may* wish to give them to you rather than sell them, thereby avoiding capital gains tax.

Income requirements. If he or she has substantial assets but cannot afford to give up income from them, he or she *may* wish to establish a charitable remainder annuity trust for himself or herself and your organization. (This will probably give him or her a fixed income for life. At his or her death, the balance of the trust assets will go to your organization.)

Tax situation. The possibilities are almost endless here. Visit with an attorney friend.

One additional thought about how much to ask for: If you're uncertain, try to err on the high side. Donors are almost *never* offended by being asked for too much (in fact, they are usually flattered). And if you do ask for too much, your donor can always suggest a smaller amount. On the other hand, donors are frequently offended by being asked for too little. A common reaction is, "So that's all they think I'm worth!"

The mechanics of prospect evaluation are best accomplished in a committee setting. Ideally, the committee should consist of people with a large number of contacts — bankers, attorneys, merchants, coaches, physicians, insurance salesmen, real estate brokers, CPA's, etc. If you pick the right people for your committee, they will give you many excellent insights. You may be able to call these people as volunteers and ask them to meet with you monthly or quarterly. Large fund-raising organizations typically have a standing "prospect evaluation committee" staffed by a full-time development officer.

A prospect identification/evaluation card is a helpful, almost indispensable tool in this whole process. A model card is shown in Figure 3-5 at the end of this chapter.

CULTIVATING PROSPECTS

Prospects, like peach trees, almost never produce to their potential unless they are carefully cultivated. It is a demanding, sometimes difficult process, but a rewarding one. Fund raisers define cultivation in several ways, but let us say here that cultivation is the sum total of activities that convince prospects that a given charity is worthy of their financial support and that lead them, ultimately, to make a contribution.

Cultivation is primarily an educational process accomplished, ideally, with a consummate sense of salesmanship. In the case of small gifts, prospects may be cultivated at the same time they are asked. Door-to-door solicitation is a case in point. It usually involves a friendly, neighborly greeting, the exchange of some amenities, the projection of a pleasing personality, and *then* a request for a contribution. Well-executed direct mail pieces work much the same way. It's best, of course, if the prospect has *some* background about the organization — perhaps via a news story published in a local paper — but it isn't imperative. People have been known to give — $5, $10 — without it.

If, however, you hope to attract large gifts from individuals, substantial advanced planning and months, even years of cultivation activities are often necessary. Some prospects will not give until they are virtually positive that the charity is a sound philanthropic investment. This knowledge can only be secured in a long-term relationship. (All of this, of course, pertains to soliciting gifts directly from individual donors. But one must remember that gifts from corporate and foundation donors are based on decisions made by individuals, whose interest also can be cultivated with similar techniques.)

It might be well to say what cultivation is *not*. It is not a series of extravagant, pre-giving "bribes" (dinners, favors, gifts, trips, deals) designed to make the prospect feel obligated. It is not a shopping list of commitments that come due when the gift comes in. It is not, in fact, an agreement to deliver on promises of any kind other than those that naturally and properly accompany charitable giving. Be extremely wary of any prospect who makes demands and for whom charitable intent seems to be a distant, idealistic notion. Contributions from such individuals are almost never worthwhile, and a satisfactory relationship with them is seldom possible.

The following "cultivation canons" have proven to be realistic, functional, and effective.

- Earn your prospects' friendship. Take a sincere interest in them. Get to know and appreciate them.

- Be prepared to give as well as to receive — to give of your time, patience, and trust.

- Help prospects understand that if they contribute to your organization, they will benefit by becoming more fulfilled and complete human beings. In the final analysis, giving is an ennobling, spiritual experience. Help your prospects come to this realization.

- Convince your prospects in a quiet way — through actions more than words — that the objectives of your organization are worthy of their support, and that they translate into practical, measurable results — a better school, bigger hospital, cleaner community, healthier world, etc.

- Demonstrate to your prospects that you and your associates believe in what you are doing — that you are committed, competent, and, again, worthy of their support.

- Make your organization meaningful to your prospects in *their* frames of reference, on *their* scales of values. If, for example, you are seeking funds for a hospital, and geriatrics is your prospect's special interest, talk about geriatrics — not about your shiny-new maternity ward.

Specifically, what steps are involved in cultivation?

Let's assume that you are in charge of fund raising for a small, private college. The college operates a special school for learning-disabled children. One of your priority projects is to raise $3,500 to buy visual aids for the school. Items needed include slide and motion picture projectors, hearing aid devices, and a library of films, pictures, and demonstration models.

You have identified a Mr. Hillman as a top prospect to contribute the $3,500. He is a successful, retired automobile dealer in your town who has been active in community affairs. He once headed up a local Heart Fund drive. How do you cultivate him? The following is a suggested course of action (it must, of course, be adjusted as individual circumstances warrant).

- Take a sincere interest in Mr. Hillman. Find out more about him — number of children, Mrs. Hillman, hobbies, schedule, health, accomplishments, close friends, birth place, education, religious and political persuasions, etc.

- Put him on the college's mailing list for materials that should interest him: newsletter published by the school of business, calendar of upcoming events, evening school class schedule, etc.

- Send him an article about the school for learning-disabled children, and include a brief, "thought you would be interested" cover letter from the college president.

- Have the president call him a week or so later and invite him to the campus for lunch. The president should offer to pick him up at his home. (A mutual friend of both Mr. Hillman and the president would be helpful here. He could extend the invitation to Mr. Hillman at the president's request, and attend the luncheon himself to make introductions and facilitate conversation.)

- At the luncheon, talk in a low-key way about the college's accomplishments and needs. *Listen* to what Mr. Hillman has to say, and try to "read" his reactions.

- After lunch, take Mr. Hillman on a tour of the campus, including the school for learning-disabled children. Let him talk with the teachers and meet the students. In an easy, careful way mention the important work of the school and the progress the students are making. Again, "read" his reactions.

- About a week after Mr. Hillman's visit, have the president send him a letter in the vein of "it was nice to have you here."

- Continue to send Mr. Hillman material of interest. (You should have some fresh insights as a result of his visit.)

- Invite him to be the president's guest at a campus activity you believe he would enjoy (play, sports events, lecture, exhibit, etc.).

- Sincerely seek his advice and counsel on matters about which he is qualified to speak. You could, for example, invite him to speak to a business class about how to operate a successful automobile dealership.

- If the signals have been neutral or positive to this point, make an appointment with him to ask for the $3,500.

Obviously, cultivation is never this cut and dried. You will encounter mixed responses and disappointments along the way. Mr. Hillman's health may not permit him to visit the campus. He may feel uncomfortable with young people. He may be an inept speaker. There are many different possibilities.

It is important — even essential — for Mr. Hillman to sense that you plan to ask for the contribution before you actually do so. This is a necessary, desirable part of cultivation. Some fund raisers nurture the notion that they can ambush prospects. This is a sure-fire way to fail.

Once Mr. Hillman senses that you plan to ask for a contribution, you will probably get one of three signals: 1) "No, I'm not interested" (this can be communicated in a variety of ways, but often takes the form of a refusal to see you); 2) "Yes, I'm interested" (he may well take the initiative by talking about a contribution); or 3) silence — that is, neither a "yes" nor "no" (this may be interpreted as a positive sign, since the prospect may well be saying to himself, "I'm willing to listen to what he has to say.")

If the signal is negative, you can take some comfort in the fact that Mr. Hillman, by being forthright with you, is not going to waste your time. You are then free to move quickly to the next name on your list.

Be Immortal.

If you could look into the eyes of generations yet to come, you would be there.

Because immortality lies not in the things you leave behind, but in the people that your life has touched, for good or bad.

By including the American Cancer Society in your will, you can have a powerful effect on those who come after you.

You see, cancer *is* beatable. The survival rate for all cancers is already approaching 50% in the United States.

You'll be leaving behind a legacy of life for others. And that is a beautiful way of living forever yourself.

AMERICAN CANCER SOCIETY ®

For more information, call your local ACS unit or write to the
American Cancer Society, 4 West 35th Street, New York, NY 10001.

Figure 3-1. Model case statement (Reprinted with the permission of The American Cancer Society, Inc.)

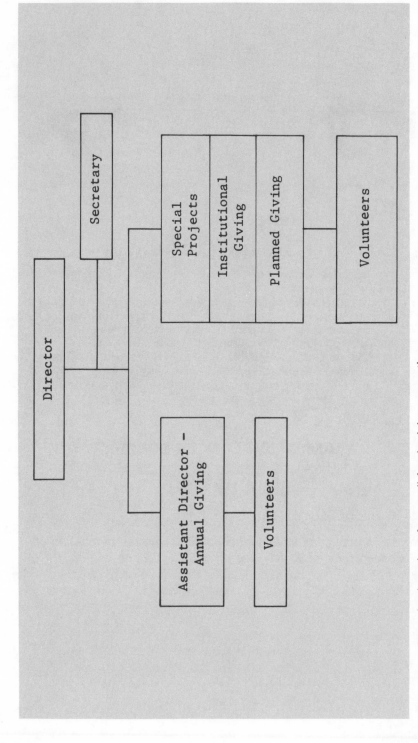

Figure 3-2. Organization chart for small fund-raising operation

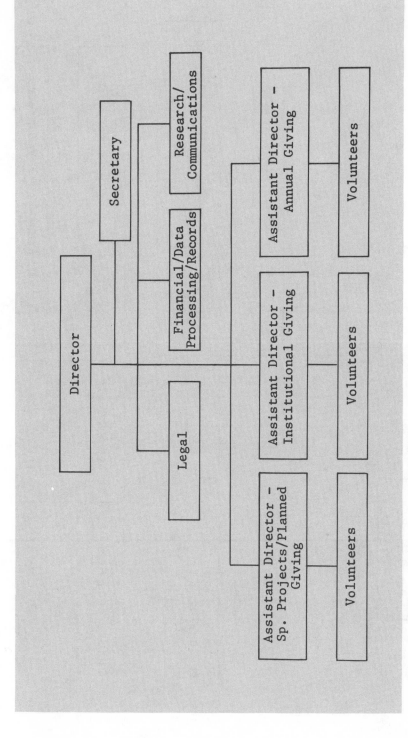

Figure 3-3. Organization chart for medium-sized fund-raising operation

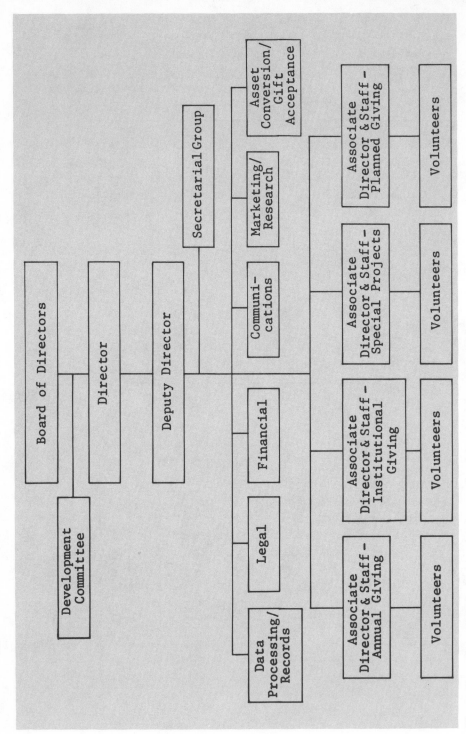

Figure 3-4. Organization chart for large-sized fund-raising operation

```
PROSPECT IDENTIFICATION/EVALUATION CARD  Name _____

Address _____ City _____ State ____ Zip ____ Phone ( ) _____

Age ____ Occupation _____ Health Condition _____ Religion _____

Marital Status: ( )Married    ( )Single    ( )Widow(er)    ( )Divorced

Spouse's Name and Age _____ Condition of Spouse's Health _____

Children's Names and Ages _____

Prospect's Memberships (Rotary, etc.) _____

Prospect's Honors, Recognition, etc. _____

Aprox. Annual Income $ _____ Est. Net Worth $ _____ Political Pref. _____

List Assets (securities, real estate, etc.) _____

Is any of this property highly appreciated?  If so, specify _____

Has prospect given to other charities?  If so, which ones/how much? _____

                    Prospect's Attorney/Accountant _____

Prospect's Interests and Hobbies _____

Special Qualities, Needs, Problems Relating to Prospect _____
```

Figure 3-5. Prospect identification/evaluation card

4 FRI ASKING TECHNIQUES AND TOOLS

This chapter introduces, explains, and evaluates the four basic asking techniques and the communication tools associated with them. Application of the techniques and tools to actual asking situations receives special, independent attention in the next chapter.

IN-PERSON TECHNIQUE

In-person asking consistently produces more and larger contributions than any other solicitation technique. Unfortunately, some fund raisers avoid it simply because they lack the confidence to look a prospect in the eye and ask. They prefer to ask *in absten-tia,* usually by means of a letter or brochure. Result: They develop few new contacts, miss out on opportunities to speak personally for their cause, and raise far less money than they otherwise would. Granted, in-person asking is not the most comfortable way to ask. It does, however, get easier with practice. Moreover, once you master it, you have access to rewards available in no other way.

Fund raisers who make appeals face-to-face with their prospects have three major advantages. 1) *Urgency and commitment.* Their personal presence tells prospects that the matter at hand is an important one to which the fund raisers are clearly, sincerely committed. It also tells prospects that the fund raisers regard them as people worthy of personal attention. These factors make for a positive beginning — before a word is spoken. 2) *Optimum, responsive communication.* Face-to-face asking gives fund raisers the enormous advantage of asking with their total being — voice, eyes, mannerisms — and all that they mean in terms of conviction, sincerity, charm, and persuasiveness. Such fund raisers have the advantage of receiving feedback from prospects, so they can tailor their presentations for maximum impact. 3) *Pressure.* It's hard to say "no" to another human being whose cause is just, who has appealed to your noblest instincts, and who is only three feet away. Some of us can be ogres when it comes to turning down an appeal by mail, over TV, or even on the telephone. But the person who asks us face to face is a force to be reckoned with!

If you have a small prospect market or a large volunteer force, you may be able to ask all of your prospects in person — an ideal situation. The pastor of a small congregation, for example, could probably manage a personal appeal to each parishioner. Many fund raisers find, however, that they must limit in-person asking to those most likely to give the largest gifts. Big universities, as a case in point, may have as many as 200,000 alumni. Obviously, only a fraction of these can be asked in person.

Good fund-raising etiquette demands that individual prospects (as opposed to foundations and corporations) be asked in person when you are asking for a large gift — one of several thousand dollars or more, or when your prospect is a distinguished individual who deserves your personal attention, particularly if he or she is conveniently available to you. It would clearly be bad form, for example, to send a solicitation letter to a prominent local physician asking him for a $5,000 contribution. That appeal should be made in person.

The communication tools appropriate for use with the in-person asking technique range from nothing more than the fund raiser's voice and sense of salesmanship to elaborate, custom-designed slide presentations and written requests. Remember, however, that the very fact that you take the time and make the effort to prepare materials of *some* kind is likely to impress prospects favorably. They may well say to themselves, "This fellow has done his homework — must be serious about this thing."

Suggested in-person asking tools and guidelines for their use are presented in the paragraphs that follow.

Charts. These can enhance almost any in-person presentation. They help to focus attention and to move speaker and listener from point to point in a logical, orderly fashion. Use type of 18 points or larger, and limit your text to key words. If you don't have access to a good typesetting device, sign painter, or free-hand letterer, type the charts in a clean, bold, sans serif face in the largest size available (the Orator face is excellent), then have a printer enlarge them photographically. You get a bonus with this approach — the unenlarged typewritten sheets which you can give the prospect as a handout. They will serve as an excellent summary of the entire presentation.

Charts and other visual aids (photographs, maps, diagrams, tables, illustrations) are especially helpful if you are asking for money for a complex or technical subject. Take care, however, that visual aids do not dominate the presentation. Concentrate on the prospect, not on the aids.

A graphically effective chart that makes good use of key words is shown in Figure 4-1 at the end of this chapter.

Written requests. Sometimes called "proposals," these are prepared in many different formats, and their content varies widely. Almost all, however, share a common purpose: to help sell projects to prospects.

For in-person asking, the written request is properly used after the presentation, as a reinforcement device and decision-making document. If, for example, you are asking for a large gift — $10,000 or more — or if the project is an involved one that requires the study of several people (including attorneys, family members, and financial advisers), you are not likely to get an answer in the meeting. Also, if you are asking for a corporate or foundation gift, you may have to wait for the decision of a board of directors or some other governing body. It is under these circumstances that the written request is most useful.

If the prospect responds favorably during the presentation, you might be well advised to keep the written request in your brief-case. Why? There is safety in generalities: Written detail, which is subject to being shown to others, may diminish rather than enhance your project's appeal to the donor and his or her advisers.

Some fund raisers go to substantial expense to prepare plush, full-color written requests. *Don't do it!* Most prospects look for substance, not ornamentation. You can produce attractive, functional, economical written requests by printing a year's supply of page-layout sheets in one color, and then printing the text for individual requests, as they come along, in black ink on those layout sheets. Stick to standard page size (8½" x 11"), and use an economical binding system that allows for changing pages. Two different styles of layout sheets, with text imprinted, are shown in Figures 4-2 and 4-3 at the end of this chapter.

There is an ongoing, spirited discussion among fund raisers as to the ideal length of a written request. Some say it should not exceed one or two pages. Others argue convincingly for at least 10 pages, sometimes backed by appendices.

The "two-track" approach is a good solution. The first "track" — a one-page summary up front — answers the argument of those who say all the prospect really needs — and reads — is a quick, clear overview. The second "track" — a 10- or 12-page in-depth treatment of the project — answers the argument of those who say that you only have one "shot" at the prospect, so you must tell your whole story.

The major sections for a model two-track written request are presented and described in the paragraphs that follow.

- Keep the **cover** simple, functional, in good taste. Figure 4-4, at the end of this chapter, shows a well designed solid-front request cover. You may, however, prefer a window cover that displays the title (from the title page), thus making it possible to identify the request quickly by name.

- On the **title page,** include title of project, date prepared, and name of submitting organization. Give careful thought to the title. It should set the tone and scope of the project, and make some kind of promise to the reader. Here are two good examples: 1) "The J. John Doe Food and Fiber Institute: Discovering and Implementing Practical Solutions to Immediate Problems — A Request for Funding Support," and 2) "Request for Funds for a New Lodge at Apple Dell Girls' Camp: An Important Investment in Our Community's Future."

A model title page is shown in Figure 4-5 at the end of this chapter.

- In a one-page **summary,** introduce the project (including why it is important and what it will accomplish), ask for the money (if you will accept partial funding support, so state), tell how and when the work will be accomplished, and give the qualifications of your organization to do the work.

  An effective one-page summary is shown in Figure 4-6.

- Define **the need;** tell why the project is necessary. Give just enough detail to establish credibility. Tone is important here. Don't talk about problems. Talk, rather, about opportunities. Help the prospect to see how he or she and your organization, working together, can make a contribution to society.

  Opening paragraphs from a well-written "Need" section are presented in Figure 4-7.

- Unveil your plan for **meeting the need** by accomplishing the proposed project. Radiate confidence and enthusiasm. This is your chance to impress the prospect with your vision and ability to plan, organize, and manage. If you have already, on your own, taken steps to help meet the need, say so. In California, for example, a group of parents was seeking funds for playground equipment. They pointed out to prospects that they had spent the last six Saturdays preparing the site. Duly impressed, their prospects gave.

"Meeting the Need" should answer at least the following questions. • When will the project begin, what are its key mileposts, and when will it end? • What tasks are involved and how will they be accomplished? • How will the project be organized, where will it be conducted, and who will direct it? • Who will have overall project responsibility, and who will disburse the funds?

- Tell of the **expected results** if the project is funded and carried through to completion. Take pains not to promise too much. Most donors don't expect their contributions to reform the world. They are satisfied if what they give helps even a small group of people in a meaningful way.

- Provide a detailed tabulation of the projected **budget,** income, and expenditures. Be sure to include financial support provided by your organization, even if it's in the form of personnel, facilities, equipment, supplies, etc. This is important, because it is to your advantage to tell your prospects that you believe enough in the project to commit your own resources to it. Above all, make your budget *realistic.* If you pad it or if you are too conservative, you will lose credibility in the eyes of your prospect (foundations are especially perceptive about budgets). If your project is funded and the budget is unrealistic, ultimately both the project and your relationship with the donor will suffer.

A model budget is shown in Figure 4-8.

- If your organization is particularly well qualified for the project because of extensive **related experience** and success with similar projects, this is the place to speak out. For example, a small college seeking travel funds for its debate team proudly — and properly — tells prospects about its string of three regional debate championships.

- Ordinarily, **personnel** can be covered in "Meeting the Need." If, however, your project involves several people in key positions, you may want to present their resumés in a separate section. Even if you take this approach, keep the resumés short and to the point. This is not the time or place for ego trips. Short but informative resumés are shown in Figure 4-9.

- Sometimes it is more comfortable — and credible — to have others speak for you. So tell the prospect **what others say.** This section consists of statements in support of your organization or project. Get the permission of the individuals involved to use their statements, and include their names and titles. Avoid crediting statements to faceless people, such as "community leader" or "food franchise executive."

- Consider writing a one-page, in-a-nutshell listing of the principal features of **your organization.** It's a convenient, readable way to handle important but basic information. A model "In Brief" listing is shown in Figure 4-10.

Slide-sound shows. You have two choices here: 1) Put together a show specifically for the project at hand, or 2) use an existing, off-the-shelf show that deals with your organization in general terms.

Custom-made, professionally produced slide-sound shows are expensive. Consequently, they can be justified only if you have a large dollar goal and you expect to present the show to several "blue chip" prospects. They can, however, be extremely effective: The combination of strong, full-color images, music, sound effects, and skillful narration can get at the very circuitry of human emotion.

It's possible, of course, for you to produce your own show. If you are inexperienced at it, you might begin with Eastman Kodak's excellent publication, "Planning and Producing Slide Programs," then visit with a scriptwriter, photographer and sound engineer.

A large university produced a custom-made slide-sound show not only for a particular project, but for a particular prospect. It involved a major campus complex to be named after the prospect, and included mockups of the buildings displaying the prospect's name. It paid off — to the tune of $4 million.

Off-the-shelf shows will help introduce an organization, set tone, communicate values, and give background. They can be worthwhile, especially if your prospect is not familiar with your organization. Resist the temptation to use a dated show — one over three or four years old. You won't get away with it (fashions, makeup, and hair style change too fast), and you'll come off looking — well, tacky.

If you use a slide-sound show, custom-made or off-the-shelf, make certain that it does not dominate the presentation. Allow ample time for friendly, personalized give and take — and for asking. *Never* have the show or any other tool do the asking in the in-person technique. Asking is *your* job. Otherwise, you might as well use another, less demanding solicitation technique, such as direct mail.

If the show must be travel-worthy — that is, if you plan to present it in various places to volunteers, former patients, alumni, prospects, etc. — you should consider having it transferred to videocassette format (assuming, of course, that you will have access to large-screen video playback units). This approach will eliminate the need for you to haul around an array of projection equipment, particularly if the show was prepared originally in multi-projector format. Speaking of multi-projector shows, you would do well to avoid them unless you're prepared to spend big dollars for specialized technical support.

Brochures, folders, special print media. Use these to add color, excitement, and graphic impact to your presentation. Do not use them in place of the written request described earlier. Why? Because fund-raising projects inevitably change during the period between conceptualization and completion — change in size, purpose, personnel, location, and even dollar amount. If you use the written request in the format described, you can easily, economically update your information. Brochures, folders, and special print media, on the other hand, cannot be economically updated. Invariably, fund raisers who prepare such pieces as their primary asking documents at the outset of a campaign end up reprinting them before the campaign is complete.

Of all the communication tools for in-person asking, these pieces of literature are the least important. They are nice, but not really necessary. Often their principal value is internal — they force decision makers to commit themselves in writing to policies, procedures, objectives, schedules, etc. If you do decide to prepare them, here are some time-tested guidelines.

- Focus on a single, simple message and get it into the title. Some good examples: "Hospitals Are for Helping" (for a community-wide hospital expansion campaign); "Paths to Progress for American Indians" (for a project to attract foundation funds for American Indian programs); "Time to Make a Choice" (for a campaign encouraging businessmen to contribute to a conservative, "free enterprise" college).

- Avoid "label" titles such as these: "Jonesville Community Church Fund," "Sixth Annual Alumni Campaign," "Hillsdale Boys' Club Drive." Don't exactly put you on the edge of your seat, do they?

- Use words that lend themselves to strong graphic design treatment. For example, the "Paths to Progress" piece features a series of lines (paths) disappearing into the distance under the title.

- Try, where practical, to include the magic word "you" or variations of it in the title. Some examples: "You and the Future of Flint Little League," "What You Should Know About Giving to the Church," "Why You're the Most Important Part of Atlanta's PTA."

- Keep copy brief, direct, to the point. Use tabulations and listings to break up type and facilitate easy reading.

- Emphasize *people* and how they will benefit from what you are doing.

- Avoid extremes in color, typography, and size. If, for example, you make a brochure 3¾" x 8½", it will easily fit into a #10 envelope, and you can use it as a mail-answering piece or in other kinds of correspondence.

- Include a coupon to encourage prospect response. A model coupon is shown in Figure 4-11 at the end of this chapter.

- Hire a good graphic designer. If the piece is worth doing at all, it's worth professional design. Fees vary, of course, but plan on spending at least a few hundred dollars on design.

Pledge card. If your prospect answers "yes" during the meeting, but is not prepared to write you a check for the full amount, *have him or her fill out a pledge card.* (See Figure 4-12.) This document is invaluable, because it helps you to:

- Commit the prospect to make the gift.

- Set the amount to be contributed.

- Establish whether the gift is to be restricted to a particular project or used for general purposes.

- Set a payment schedule.

- Prepare the way for follow-up.

Even if the gift is to be given in deferred form, such as an annuity trust, the pledge card is still useful, simply because it formalizes the prospect's promise to give.

You should carefully file and maintain completed pledge cards, so that they are easily available for follow-up purposes. (Note that the card shown in Figure 4-12 fits into a standard file.)

If you have access to a data processing system, you should consider entering pledges into your computer file, and then periodically reviewing them — via a printout — for follow-up action.

GROUP TECHNIQUE

Under the right circumstances, this approach is next in effectiveness to in-person asking. Its great strength is social and peer pressure.

Let's look at the group technique in action. In an Illinois city of 50,000, a respected business leader held a dinner for 25 of the city's most successful businessmen. In his formal, written invitations to them, he said he wanted to discuss "a matter of importance to the city's future." He greeted them at the door, and, after they had eaten, he stood up and said this:

"Gentlemen, I want you to know that I appreciate your attendance here this evening. You know that there's no such thing as a free lunch — or dinner! I think you know, too, that our city swimming pool needs to be repaired and enlarged. In its present condition, it's unsafe for our children. The city doesn't have the tax revenues to do the job — and won't have for several years. I know *we* have the means — and I believe *we* have the desire — to do something about it. I will contribute a dollar for every dollar each of you contributes. You must, however, contribute a minimum of $500. What do you say?"

This bold, talented and selfless fund raiser had arranged for two of the businessmen in attendance to lead off by pledging gifts of $1,000 each. Predictably, the others followed suit. Pledge cards were completed by every businessman before the evening ended.

Too much pressure, you say? Perhaps. Clearly, in some circumstances, a lower-key approach would be safer and more appropriate. You could, for example, hold a luncheon or dinner, explain your project and the benefits it will offer your community, pass out pledge cards, and then *invite* those in attendance to contribute. If you perform well, a few will pledge then and there, and a few others will mail in their cards to you. Some, of course, will not respond. You should solicit these in-person or by telephone.

The group technique is most likely to succeed when three conditions exist: 1) The person who asks is respected, influential, and agreeably aggressive; 2) the group is united by religion, politics, profession, national origin, or some other strong element of commonality; and 3) the project or cause is one in which the group deeply believes. (Sometimes the strong element is adversity. For example, the parents and wives of American servicemen missing in action or unaccounted for in Vietnam gave freely of their own funds — and were effective in raising funds from others — in support of their search for their loved ones.)

The communication tools appropriate for the group technique, in addition to the pledge card, include all of those recommended for the in-person technique.

TELEPHONE

The telephone is the third most effective solicitation technique. It is best used in intensive, one- or two-night calling campaigns known variously as "phonothons," "telefunds," and "fonathons." Unquestionably, these campaigns enable you to reach large numbers of people economically and with reasonably good impact. In addition, they minimize the time and effort required of volunteer workers — an important consideration for many organizations.

If you have only a few people to call, you can, of course, ask by telephone without organizing a calling campaign. If you only have a few prospects to ask, and if they are available locally, you might as well use the in-person technique. It will increase your chances of success.

Contributions given in response to telephone solicitation range from a few dollars to as much as $100,000 or more. It is, of course, inappropriate to ask for large sums of money by telephone. One possible exception: special campaigns featuring celebrity volunteers who call "blue chip" prospects. Another is when you absolutely cannot solicit the prospect in person.

Conducting a phonothon — the preferred term — is not difficult. It does, however, require substantial organization, detail work, and followup. Here are the steps.

- Compile a calling list. Research the names, addresses and telephone numbers of people who could reasonably be expected to contribute to your cause. In the case of educational institutions, for example, alumni and parents of students are ideal prospects. Design and print phonothon cards (Figure 4-13), and enter on them the information from your list. (The card shown in Figure 4-13 is a basic one. Institutions with years of phonothon experience use sophisticated cards with computer-printed entries. Some even list past giving records, name of spouse, and whether or not the prospect works for a matching gift company.) Note that the card shown in Figure 4-13 consists of two parts. The top part is a "pledge reminder/thank you" that the volunteer fills in and signs if the prospect pledges. It is designed so that the address will show through a window envelope, and it is mailed to the pledgee. The bottom part is a "record of call" that the volunteer fills in, and the organization retains.

- Recruit one volunteer caller for every 40 prospects you want to contact in a single evening of calling. Get more than you need, because you will probably have some last-minute dropouts. Recruit from among those who are friends of your cause — past givers, loyal supporters, former officers, etc. If you have a choice, opt for salesmen, professionals, and people with good speaking skills. Recruit them in person or by telephone.

- Locate a facility with a large number of telephones, and reserve it. Banks and stock brokerage firms are excellent. Many will make their facilities available free of charge as a good-will gesture. Avoid Fridays, weekends, and holidays.

- Two weeks before the phonothon, call the volunteers and give them a date and place. Ask them to be there at 6 p.m. sharp. Tell them you will serve a box lunch or some kind of "packaged" dinner (something self-contained with napkins, plastic utensils, etc.) Ask them to plan to stay until 9:30 p.m.

- Five days before the phonothon, send the volunteers a friendly post card reminding them of the phonothon date, place, and time.

- Two nights before the phonothon, call the volunteers and confirm their plans to attend. Dropouts will surface now; you should have allowed for them.

- Arrive at the facility a half-hour early. Tape a "welcome" sign to the front door. Make sure everything is in order. Put the phonothon cards and dinner by each phone. Set up any visual aids you intend to use.

- Greet the volunteers warmly at the door. To help with names and introductions, you may wish to have them fill out identification cards and pin them on.

- When all the volunteers have arrived, greet them as a group, thank them for coming, and invite them to begin eating.

- When they are nearly finished eating (about 6:30), begin your orientation. Put them at ease by being relaxed, almost casual (they need this, especially if it's their first experience with telephone solicitation). Tell them how much you hope to raise during the evening. They should already be converted to your cause, but touch briefly on it. Sample: "What you do this evening can make a real difference — a lasting difference — in the quality of education available to Central College students." Introduce them to the phonothon card, and tell them how to fill it out. (Some phonothon directors use a large blowup of the card for this purpose. Others provide a handout giving step-by-step instructions. A few institutions use slide shows or filmstrips.) Ask them to group the phonothon cards into piles, depending on the results of each call: one pile for "not home," another for "pledged," another for "wrong number," etc. (See bottom part of card, Figure 4-13.)

- Review the elements of a good telephone approach. Tell them to relax, be themselves, and speak naturally. Read a model approach to them — something like this:

"Hello, Pat Johnson?" (Response.) "This is Kelly Walker calling. I understand that you graduated from Central College in 1978...is that right?" (Response.)

"I'm calling with a group of phonothon volunteers, and we need your help. We're raising money to enable Central to continue its great work. Right now, the fieldhouse expansion is a special need. Can we count on you for a contribution...say $25?'' (It's important to suggest a specific amount, or at least a giving range. Most prospects hesitate to make a specific pledge until they know the amount you have in mind. Wait for the response. If it's positive, thank the individual, confirm her or his address, and hang up. If it's negative, then proceed as follows.) ''I can certainly understand how you feel — things are tight for many of us these days. We're not really looking for a large contribution. If it would be easier, perhaps you could pay some now and the balance later. What do you think?'' (Response. Quite often, the individual will say something like, ''Well...maybe I could give you half now and half in a couple of months.'' Your response might then be, ''That's great, Pat. We appreciate your generosity.'' You then confirm the address. If, however, the prospect still resists, it's best to back off. Try to end on a positive note: ''It's been nice talking with you, Pat. Perhaps you can help us another time. Have a good evening.'')

- Ask if there are any questions, then tell them to begin calling (it should be about 6:50 by now.) It's good strategy to arrange the cards so that the inexperienced volunteers will call the most promising prospects first — individuals who have given in the past or who you know are favorable to your program. Positive responses at the outset will boost confidence.

- Some fund raisers use cowbells or other noisemakers to build volunteer espirit. Volunteers actuate them every time they receive a pledge. They help!

- Circulate among the volunteers to see how they are doing. Offer suggestions, give encouragement, and be available to answer questions.

- Try to keep a running total of pledges received. Post the total periodically for all to see.

- At the end of the evening (about 9:15), announce the grand total, collect the cards, and warmly thank each volunteer.

- Ask the volunteers to sign "Thanks for the use of your desk" cards or table tents (Figure 4-14), and leave them on the desks they used. Also, send a thank-you letter within a few days to the individual who let you use the facility. These are little things, but they can make the difference between a "yes" and a "no" the next time you want to use the facility.

- Mail the pledge reminder slips that very evening, or, the next day at the latest. Include a self-addressed remittance envelope.

- Send an upbeat reminder letter to those who have not sent in their contribution after a month. (A suggested letter is shown in Figure 4-15.) Institutions with sophisticated phonothon programs use a reminder form with computer-printed entries. This is not necessarily more effective, just more efficient. You may wish to take a softer reminder approach than that shown in Figure 4-15. You could, for example, begin your letter by thanking the individual for his or her pledge and giving a progress report on the campaign. You would then conclude by encouraging the pledgee to send in his or her contribution. If the pledgees don't respond to your letter, regardless of the approach you take, write them off. Further effort is probably not justified. If 60 percent or more of those who pledged pay, you've done well.

Some fund raisers effectively combine direct mail with phonothons. The approach is to send a letter three weeks before the phonothon to everyone on the calling list. The letter introduces the organization, explains the need for contributions and how they will be used, announces that the individual will be called, and concludes with a P.S. like this, "In the event we are unable to reach you by telephone, a remittance envelope is enclosed for your convenience." There are three vital advantages to this approach: 1) It prepares prospects for your call and gives them helpful advance information (some people *never* give to a charity until they check it out); 2) it reduces the number of people your volunteers have to call, because some will give in direct response to the mailer; and 3) it ensures that you will reach virtually everyone on your calling list — if not by phone, then by mail.

The mechanics of a phonothon — the forms, procedures, and instructions — are perhaps the most difficult part of the technique. But outside suppliers offer those mechanics as a packaged system, tested and ready to use. (One of these is the FRI Phonothon System.)

Here is a quick look at three successful, real-life phonothon campaigns that may help you get started.

- Directors of a center for retarded children were seeking funds for new recreational equipment. They conducted a phonothon at the center and had parents of the children make the calls. The phonothon was preceded by a television interview with the directors over a local station. Amount raised: $1,175.

- A college athletic director wanted to raise additional funds for athletic recruiting. He asked coaches and star players to call season ticket holders and alumni who had been athletes (this involved some long-distance). Amount raised: $4,800.

- The adviser to a high school band needed travel funds for a trip to the Tournament of Roses Parade. Three hours before the phonothon, the band appeared in a promotional parade with signs reading, "You'll Be Hearing More From Us Tonight!" Parents of the band members and teachers made the calls. Amount raised: $1,400.

DIRECT MAIL

Consult 10 different experts about how best to succeed with direct mail and you're likely to receive 10 distinctly different sets of instructions. The experts do agree on one thing, however: Direct mail is one of the least effective fund-raising solicitation techniques in terms of the number of gifts received per prospect solicited. In fact, if 5 percent of the prospects you solicit by direct mail respond with a contribution, you're doing exceptionally well.

None of this means, however, that direct mail is not worth your while. The explanation? There is strength in numbers. Direct mail reaches millions of people with billions of messages. And increasingly those messages are not wild shots in the dark, but meticulously aimed appeals that hit their targets with sharp-shooter accuracy.

The intent of this section is not to make you an expert in direct mail (that would require a separate volume), but to show you how to get started, and to offer some practical guidelines.

Address lists. Whether a direct mail solicitation succeeds or fails is determined principally by the quality of its address list. If, for example, the list contains the names and addresses of people who are sympathetic to your cause, your mailing will probably succeed. If, on the other hand, your list is a haphazard collection of names mixed with high hopes, your mailing will probably not pay for itself.

You can rent address lists of the names of people who would reasonably be expected to contribute to your cause (list rental is, in fact, big business in the United States). If, for example, you are seeking funds to establish a premedical scholarship program, you might want to rent a "doctors and dentists" address list. Several firms offer them, including one that has a 500,000-name list broken down by medical specialty. "Direct Mail List — Rates and Data," a publication of Standard Rate and Data Service, Inc. (3004 Glenview Rd., Wilmette, IL 60091; phone 312-256-6067), is the place to start. This directory, available at many libraries, compiles, organizes, classifies, and arranges all known, available opportunities for using the mail for advertising. It is, in effect, a catalog of mailing lists that you can rent and use to address your solicitation mailings. "Direct Mail List — Rates and Data," which is published every other month, also includes a section giving the names, addresses, and phone numbers of list brokers, compilers, and managers. Brokers often can provide excellent advice on which may be the most responsive lists, and they'll provide that advice without cost to you. (They make their money from a commission paid by the list owner when you rent a list through the broker.)

If you are just getting started in direct mail, you may be better off compiling your own address list. This is especially appropriate if you intend to solicit prospects who are uniquely identified with your organization. For example, who is in a better position to prepare a list of alumni prospects than the fund-raising director of the college from which they graduated?

The following are rich sources of names for do-it-yourself lists.

- *Past donors.* These are your best prospects, of course, because they have already demonstrated their loyalty. Don't make the mistake, however, of soliciting potential "large gift" donors year after year by mail. They should be asked in person.

- *People you have served.* Think of the people your organization has helped in some way — educated, counseled, operated on, toured with — they are ideal direct mail prospects.

- *People you will serve in the future.* Community college fund raisers would do well to list the names of parents of local high school seniors; hospital fund raisers, the names of heads of middle- and upper-income households in the community.

- *People who share your interests.* Two examples: 1) The director of a drug-counseling center in need of funds listed local doctors, psychologists, counselors, social workers, and judges; 2) a Little League coach who needed funds for baseball equipment listed local high school and college coaches plus the players and owners of his city's professional baseball team.

The mailer. If you've looked in your mail box lately, you know direct mailing pieces come in all sizes, colors, and styles. Basically, however, they are of two kinds: self-mailers and envelope mailers.

A self-mailer is a folder, brochure, flyer, or other print-media piece sent without an envelope. The address is imprinted on, or stuck to, the mailer proper. These are popular with many fund raisers because of their low cost. They are economical to print, process, and mail. As a rule, however, they are less effective than envelope mailers. Unless they are well designed, they are not likely to command the attention given to a well-executed envelope mailer. Their most serious drawback, however, is that you cannot easily include a remittance envelope with them. (It *can* be done. You can, for example, staple or glue the remittance envelope inside. If your quantities are large enough to make it economical, you can order self-mailers from specialty printers with ingenious tear-off envelopes.)

If you use a self-mailer, make it large enough to attract attention and to be inviting, and be sure to include a convenient clip-and-mail coupon to facilitate prospect response.

Envelope mailers, in their simplest form, consist of an outside envelope, letter, and remittance envelope. The more elaborate ones include brochures or folders, and some of the gimmicky ones add such things as seed packets, unused stamps, and miniature pencils.

Opinion varies on how best to handle each component in an envelope mailer, but the following guidelines have the most defenders.

- *Outside envelope.* Use a #10 (4¹/₈'' x 9½''), white, medium-stock quality, window envelope, and print the regular name and address of your organization in the normal return-address position. Teaser copy (a statement on the front that makes a promise or otherwise piques interest) may or may not be a good idea. If you can come up with something exciting while avoiding overstatement, it should be helpful. Here's a simple teaser that worked well: ''Inside...an important message for you from Billy Casper.'' Some authorities say you should not use a return address on the outside envelope. Their idea is to make the mailer look as much like a bill as possible, since almost everybody opens bills. There are two problems with this approach: 1) It violates at least the spirit of Better Business Bureau solicitation standards which rule out fund-raising literature made to look like bills, and 2) the absence of a return address makes it impossible for the United States Postal Service to return incorrectly addressed letters to you.

With a return address, you can enlist the Postal Service in helping to update your address list by printing ADDRESS CORRECTION REQUESTED on the outside envelope just below the return address. If the address is incorrect and the new address is known by the USPS, a sticker bearing the new address will be affixed to the envelope, and it will be forwarded to the intended recipient at his or her new residence. Before it is forwarded, however, a copy will be made of the envelope with the sticker, and it will be sent to you so you can make note of it. You will be charged for this service. If the address is incorrect and the new address is *not* known by the USPS, or if there is some other problem, the appropriate notation will be made on the envelope and it will be returned to you. There is *no* charge for this service.

- *Letter.* The lead is the most important part of a direct mail solicitation letter. If properly conceptualized and written, it will capture the reader's interest, make a promise of some kind, and prepare him or her to receive your message and act on it. Here are six kinds of good leads for solicitation letters. *News:* Make an announcement of some kind ("Carterville's scouts are building a new lodge, and you're invited to be part of it!"). *Narrative:* Plunge the prospect into a dramatic, interesting story ("On a chilly October evening in 1953, Virginia Stowe opened her front door and confronted a bedraggled, runaway boy who asked for a bowl of soup. He was the beginning of today's Stowe Homes for Boys"). *Question:* Involve and challenge the reader by asking a provocative question ("Do you know how many Freeburg girls won't be going to summer camp this year?"). *Itemization:* Use numbers to build credibility and get the prospect into your message ("Here are 12 practice-proved ways that Odyssey House helps kids with drug problems"). *Why/What/How:* Use a headline to answer questions your prospect could be expected to have about your organization ("How Wilson PTA Serves You and Your Child — And What to Expect in the Years Ahead"). *Startling Statement:* Grab the reader and almost force him or her to listen to what you have to say ("We're losing our minds!").

The body of the letter should build on the lead — amplify, prove, document, cite, enumerate. This is a good place to talk about *benefits* ("You'll have the satisfaction of knowing your gift is lifting young lives — today and in the years ahead"), and to marshal the support of outside spokesmen ("My seven years as Juvenile Court Judge have taught me that young people need a place to go where they feel comfortable...learn about themselves and others. That's why I enthusiastically support the club house campaign.")

Use a general, "blanket" salutation ("Dear Friend," "Dear Girl Scout Parent," etc.) if it seems right for your audience. If you're not comfortable with it (some fund raisers feel that blanket salutations reek of insincerity), don't use a salutation — get right into the letter. The best approach, of course, is to use a personalized inside address and salutation ("Dear Mr. Johnson"), but this is time consuming and expensive if you are mailing to a hundred people or so and you do not have an automatic typewriter or word-processing equipment. We have all received letters in which the body has been printed and the inside address and salutation have been added by a typist in a matching face. Most people are "on" to this approach, and it's doubtful that the special effort involved is worth it.

The concluding paragraph of the letter should summarize your appeal, issue a clear call for action, and convey a sense of urgency ("In short, Louis and his American Indian classmates need your help. And they need it *today.* Please take time *now* — while it's on your mind — to write out a check and return it in the envelope provided. Thanks!").

Some other guidelines for solicitation letters. • Use short sentences, simple words, and short paragraphs (six lines or less). • Try for a conversational style that communicates warmth, openness, friendliness. • Avoid superlatives and claims that challenge credibility. • Leave no doubt about what you want. • Remember that letters of almost any length — short, medium, long — are effective if they are well conceptualized and written. • Arrange your thoughts so that they flow logically and easily from lead to conclusion. • Always include a meaningful P.S. — these have high readership.

Solicitation letters for higher education, church, community service, and health care are shown in Figures 4-16 through 4-21 at the end of this chapter.

• *Brochures and folders.* These are best used to *show* prospects — by means of illustrations, diagrams, photographs — why they should contribute to your cause. Too often brochures and folders are simply dressed-up extensions of letters — all blow (text) and no show (illustrations, etc.). A citizens' group seeking funds to cover two dangerous irrigation ditches had the right idea. They prepared a flyer to accompany their letter containing photographs of the exposed ditches and of two young children who had drowned in them. The flyer included a sketch detailing how the ditches would be covered.

If your project is one that doesn't require visual explanation (a college scholarship fund, for example), you can easily forego a brochure or folder, and do your budget a big favor.

The guidelines for brochures, folders, and special print media for in-person asking listed earlier in this chapter also apply to similar items used in direct mail.

• *Remittance envelope.* The remittance envelope (or gift envelope) is essential for two reasons: 1) It makes it convenient for the prospect to respond; 2) its backside can carry the address label, which shows through the outside envelope window. This label also serves to identify the donor when he or she mails the remittance envelope back to you with the contribution. (Not all donors write their return address on the remittance envelope. If they send cash rather than checks, the label is your only means of identifying them.)

If the remittance envelope is to be machine-stuffed into the outside envelope, make sure it's one inch shorter and at least one-quarter inch narrower than the outside envelope.

Some organizations print a gift form on the inside flap of the remittance envelope. Most experts discourage this practice, because they feel that the back flap of the remittance envelope is too far removed from the message (letter) proper. Moreover, wallet-style remittance envelopes (those with large flaps) are expensive. Solution? Enclose a gift form with the letter. Limit the gift options on the coupon to four at the most. Research suggests that including too many options causes prospects to set the mailer aside while they think the matter over. Unfortunately, of course, they never get back to it. (One large university, which had been including check-off boxes for all 15 of its colleges, realized a substantial increase in response rate when it limited the choices to four, including a line reading "Other.")

Many direct mail specialists feel that the remittance envelope should be postage prepaid (business reply), and extensive testing generally supports them. You pay, of course, only for those envelopes actually sent back to you. It might be well, however, for you to do some testing of your own: The difference in response with and without prepaid postage in your particular circumstance may not warrant the expense.

Always print your address on the remittance envelope in the normal address position. Also, consider using colored stock — there is evidence suggesting that colored remittance envelopes have a higher return rate than white ones.

COMPUTER-ASSISTED TRANSLATION PROJECT	
PURPOSE:	DEVELOP A FAST, FAIRLY ECONOMICAL WAY TO TRANSLATE WRITTEN RUSSIAN, SPANISH, & FRENCH TO ENGLISH
ORGANIZATION:	TRANSLATION SCIENCE CENTER PERSONNEL
DIRECTOR:	J. DWIGHT JOHNSEN
LOCATION:	STATESBURG CAMPUS
SCHEDULE:	OCT 84 - COMPLETE LANGUAGE ANALYSIS
	JUL 86 - COMPLETE INITIAL PROGRAM
	JUL 87 - COMPLETE DETAILED PROGRAM
	DEC 88 - COMPLETE PRODUCTION MODEL
	JAN 89 - IMPLEMENT & REFINE
COST:	$2,450,000

Figure 4-1. Model chart

RESULTS OF STUDY

This research is expected to supply the following information and data base specifications:

(a) A generalized specification for informa-
    tion flow and directory distribution
    in a distributed data base system.

(b) Generalized specifications for security
    techniques.

(c) Generalized specifications for query
    languages and techniques.

(d) A delineation of additional problems
    needing study and research in integrat-
    ed distributed systems.

(e) A delineation of additional security
    problems needing further examination.

Figure 4-2. Written request layout sheet — style A

o Another Castledale musical organization,
  Opera Workshop, recently presented Menotti's
  <u>Amahl and the Night Visitors</u>. Workshop
  students are now preparing another major
  production, <u>Peter Pan</u>, to be presented this
  spring.

o The College's traveling troupe of musicians
  and dancers--"Showcase Castledale"--in-
  volves 30 students from ten countries whose
  presentation is keyed to the theme, "Peace
  for All Nations through Stronger Families."
  Last year the troupe traveled 3,500 miles
  in giving 74 performances at schools,
  hospitals, and other institutions in the
  mountain states.

Unquestionably, Castledale has a rich,
rewarding musical program. But the College,
and the Music Department in particular,
have pressing needs that cannot be met without the active, concerned involvement of
alumni, corporations, foundations, and individuals.

Castledale College

Figure 4-3. Written request layout sheet — style B

REQUEST

Brigham Young University

Figure 4-4. Solid-front cover for written request

VIDEODISC: CAUSING A COMMUNICATIONS
REVOLUTION IN EDUCATION

A REQUEST FOR FUNDING SUPPORT

The Development Office
Brigham Young University
Provo, Utah 84602

Figure 4-5. Title page for written request

SUMMARY

Castledale College and its Department of Continuing Education respectfully request your financial support in the amount of $4,600,000 to construct a self-contained continuing education complex that will handle present programs and future growth.

Full or partial funding is invited.

The Castledale continuing education program is now one of the largest in America, with registrations exceeding 225,000 annually. The program has quality as well as quantity, including pioneering programs in nutrition and nursing.

Unfortunately, the Department is caught in a critical space squeeze. Space for administrative functions is only about half of what it should be...regular College classroom space is not available at all during the regular school year... and the nearest hotel is miles away.

The complex, to be built on the south end of the campus, will consist of: Administrative Center ($1,400,000, 28,000 square feet), Conference Center ($2,600,000, 48,000 square feet), and Residence Center ($600,000, 17,000 square feet). Construction could begin as early as next spring if funding support were available.

The sections that follow present the need for the complex, plans to meet the need, budget, schedule, and other information to help you evaluate this request.

Figure 4-6. Summary for written request

THE NEED

The lives of Americans are being increasingly affected by scientific decisions. If we are to have a proper measure of control over how we live, and if we are to participate meaningfully in public and private matters involving energy, re-sources, transportation, and health, we must develop mature attitudes toward science.

General science courses at grade school through university levels, developed many years ago to meet the need for broadly based science educa-tion, have been helpful. But the crisis climate of the Seventies, with its direct challenge to scientific disciplines, has created an acute need for greatly increased public awareness of science in general and of sound in particular. Why specifically sound? Because it is central to so many other fields--language, music, speech, psychology, biology, architecture, physics, math--and thus provides a natural vehicle for relevant science experiences.

The need for enhanced science education and the reaction to it is everywhere evident--in the

Figure 4-7. Opening paragraphs from model "The Need" section

BUDGET

Expenses

Capital Expenses
Equipment	$ 62,200
Farm House	35,000
Sheds	11,000
Land Clearing	20,000
Roads, Fences	29,000

Operating Expenses
Salaries (fulltime & students) . .	436,000
Utilities	35,000
Supplies (seeds, fuel, plants) . .	141,800
Hardware (lumber, wire, tools) . .	34,000
Depreciation	12,000
Total Expenses	$ <u>816,000</u>

Revenue

Plot & Equipment Rentals	$ 6,000
Crops	
Beans	30,500
Peas	65,000
Lettuce	50,000
Total Revenue	$ <u>151,500</u>

Balance to be Funded . . . . $ <u>664,500</u>

Figure 4-8. Budget for written request

PERSONNEL

J. Dwight Johnsen, associate professor of languages, is CSI project director. He is the author
of Computer-Aided Translation, the work upon which
the project is based. Dr. Johnsen received his
M.A. in German from Central College in 1961 and
his Ph.D. from the University of Illinois in 1970,
where he studied Slavic languages for three years
under a NDFL Fellowship. He joined the CC faculty
in 1967. Dr. Johnsen initiated computer-aided
translation research at CC in 1968. Since then he
has received three government contracts for research and development in language theory. He has
published over twenty articles in the professional
literature.

Thomas K. Steele, assistant to Dr. Johnsen, received his M.A. from Stanford University in
Chinese and his Ph.D. from Georgetown University
in Chinese and Linguistics. He lived for three
years in Taiwan and studied for two years in
Hong Kong under a NDFL Fellowship. Dr. Steele's
professional experience includes two years as head
of language instruction for the U. S. Defense Department and three years as a translator for
Internationale, Inc. He joined Central College in
1970. His publications include over a dozen
journal articles, papers at four symposiums, and
a book, New Insights Into Chinese Linguistic
Structure.

Figure 4-9. Model personnel resumes

WEBER STATE COLLEGE IN BRIEF

The College was founded at Ogden, Utah as Weber Stake
Academy on January 7, 1889 by the Weber Stake Board of Ed-
ucation of The Church of Jesus Christ of Latter-day Saints.
The 1933 Utah Legislature established Weber as a state
junior college and placed it under control of the Utah
State Board of Education.

In 1959 the Utah Legislature authorized upper division
courses. Weber graduated its first senior class in 1963–
64. The 1969 legislature created a Utah System of Higher
Education and placed WSC under a State Board of Regents
and an Institutional Council. WSC is one of the largest
four-year baccalaureate degree-granting colleges in America.

President: Dr. Rodney H. Brady, B.S., M.B.A., University
of Utah, 1957; D.B.A., Harvard Graduate School of Business
Administration, 1966.

Campus: 375 acres, 32 buildings, plant investment of
more than $30 million. Over 88% of total building
space has been built since 1960.

Faculty: 450 men and women representing a broad spectrum
of local, state, national, and international backgrounds.
About 200 hold doctoral degrees.

Students: Nearly 10,000 students representing 43 states
and a dozen foreign countries.

Colleges: Baccalaureate degrees awarded in seven major
schools with 32 departments and a Bachelor of General
Studies. Associate degrees and one- and two-year
curriculums offered in vocational and health fields.
Quarter system: fall, winter, spring, and summer.

Figure 4-10. Representative "In Brief" listing

MEMBERSHIP APPLICATION

I want to promote athletics at Brigham Young University. Please enroll me as a member of the BYU Cougar Club.

Name _____ Address _____

City _____ State _____ Zip _____ Date _____

(Your Cougar Club contribution is a tax-exempt gift to the BYU Annual Alumni Fund and will be restricted to the Athletic Travel Fund for the purpose of recruiting athletes, according to NCAA and WAC regulations.)

Please accept my annual tax-deductible contribution of:

☐ $1,500 (Lifetime Member-
    ship; also payable @
    $500/year for three years)
☐ $500 (Golden Cougar)
☐ $100 (Regular Member)

☐ $25 (Associate Member,
    25 years of age and under)

☐ Check enclosed
☐ Bill me

Figure 4-11. Coupon to facilitate prospect response

⦿ PLEDGE CARD
THE DEVELOPMENT OFFICE

The Development Office
P.O. Box 7188 University Station
Provo, Utah 84602
(801) 374-1211, Ext. 2222

Gentlemen:
I hereby pledge to _____ the sum of $ _____. I would like my contribution to

(check one) ☐ be used for general purposes ☐ be restricted to _____.

I have enclosed $ _____, and I intend to pay any remaining balance as follows (check one):
☐ monthly ☐ quarterly ☐ semi-annually ☐ annually

Name _____ Address _____

City _____ State _____ Zip _____

Signed _____ Date _____

Comments _____

_____

Figure 4-12. Model pledge card

Castledale College
Wendover, Utah 84083

Thank you for your support of the annual fund in the amount of $_____ .

Sincerely,_____
         Volunteer Worker

[address box]

Make all address corrections within the address box above.
Please return this completed slip with your contribution.

Amount enclosed $_____
(can be paid in installments)

Please make checks payable to Castledale College.

GIFT INSTRUCTIONS

☐ Use my gift where the need is greatest.
☐ Restrict my gift to_____ .

RECORD OF CALL

1. Total Amount Pledged: $_____
   (can be paid in installments)

   Gift Instructions:
   ☐ Use where need is greatest.
   ☐ Restrict gift to _____ .

2. Call Back: ☐Line busy ☐Not home

3. Unreachable: ☐Moved ☐Wrong number
   ☐Deceased

4. Call Completed, Special Response:
   ☐Already gave
   ☐Does not wish to give this year

Figure 4-13. Phonothon card

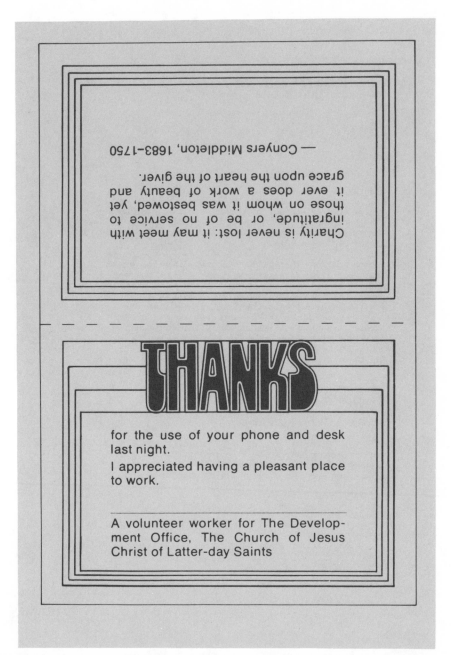

Charity is never lost: it may meet with ingratitude, or be of no service to those on whom it was bestowed, yet it ever does a work of beauty and grace upon the heart of the giver.
— Conyers Middleton, 1683-1750

THANKS

for the use of your phone and desk last night.

I appreciated having a pleasant place to work.

A volunteer worker for The Development Office, The Church of Jesus Christ of Latter-day Saints

Figure 4-14. "Thanks for Use of Your Desk" table tent

Castledale College
Wendover, Utah 84083

Frankly, we're worried.

If our records are correct, we have not yet received your pledged contribution to Castledale College. And, unfortunately, time is running out. Our Silver Anniversary Fund closes September 15th.

I hope you know that we do need your financial support, and that your gift--large or small--is welcomed and needed. The quality of Castledale's service in the years ahead will depend, in large measure, upon the support of those who believe in us...people like you.

Please take time now--while you're thinking about it--to send in your contribution.

All of us at CC appreciate your friendship and support.

Sincerely,

Brandon R. Ralphs, President

P.S. The premiere showing of CC's Silver Anniversary motion picture, "From These Beginnings," will be held August 21, 8 p.m., in Glendon Hall. Admission is free. I hope you and your family will be able to attend.

Figure 4-15. Reminder letter to phonothon pledgees

RICKS
COLLEGE

OFFICE OF THE PRESIDENT

Someone once asked a successful fund-raiser if he ever flinched at asking for money. "I did once," he confessed, "when I wasn't personally convinced of the worth of the project for which I sought funds."

Fortunately, no one at Ricks College ever needs to flinch at asking for money for Ricks projects. All of them are worthwhile in the lives of young people.

Some projects, however, have a greater potential than others to reach people in a positive way beyond the campus and beyond the present generation. That's true of the College's campaign to raise $200,000 to buy a medium-sized pipe organ for the new fine arts building.

The students who become skilled organists as a result of being able to practice on this magnificent instrument will go forth throughout the world to touch the souls of men and women through music.

Please take a moment to read the accompanying folder--it gives complete details--and then use the enclosed reply card and envelope to make your contribution.

I know you'll feel good about it.

Sincerely,

Henry B. Eyring

Henry B. Eyring, President

P.S. Our Sixth Annual Piano Festival opens on April 9. You are cordially invited to attend.

Figure 4-16. Solicitation letter (higher education)

COMMUNITY
CHRISTIAN CHURCH
Harrisburg

Dear Brother & Sister Helms:

There are many ways to ask people for money. None of them, though, is easy. But if your cause is just and you have a special feeling for the people you ask--well, that can help a lot.

As you probably heard in Sunday worship service earlier this month, Community Christian Church needs your help if it is to serve you better--more comfortably, more completely. Specifically, we would like to lay new carpet in the chapel (you'll agree, we think, that it needs it)... expand the scripture library (we're down to four Bibles!) ...and improve the sound system in the recreational hall (and you thought it was your ears all these years!).

Most of the members with whom we have spoken agree that these improvements are important and worthwhile.

The total amount needed--based on the best estimates available--is $5,700. That amount can quickly be raised if you and every other member family will contribute $65.

Please accept this invitation to join with the other member families in improving our worship facilities. You can contribute in person at the Church or, if you prefer, you can use the enclosed remittance envelope.

Thanks for all you do, in many different ways, to prosper His work here in Harrisburg.

Sincerely,

Stanley C. Hawthorne

Stanley C. Hawthorne, Pastor

P. S. We hope that all contributions can be made within sixty days so that the improvements will be complete in time for our special Easter service.

Figure 4-17. Solicitation letter (church)

Dear Friend:

Today, right now, you can take a giant step for brotherhood.
Let me tell you about it.

In half-a-dozen programs on and off campus, BYU is waging
an exceptionally effective campaign to help the American
Indian...to give him hope and to break the ages-old pattern
of poverty, disease, and despair.

The techniques being used involve everything from educational
psychologists and soil scientists to one-ton tractors and
aerial maps.

On campus, the American Indian Education Department is giving
tailor-made assistance to 500 Indian students in three academic programs expressly designed for them. Off-campus, the
University's Institute of American Indian Services is helping
Indians in agriculture, tribal government, alcoholism education, small business development--and much more.

The spirit that characterizes all of these programs is an
abiding, consuming concern for the American Indians' spiritual
and temporal welfare.

The enclosed brochure tells the whole story. I hope you'll
read it thoughtfully. And, in a few days when a volunteer
worker calls and asks you for a pledge, I hope you'll take a
giant step for brotherhood by answering yes.

Thanks!

Donald T. Nelson
Director, The Development Office

P. S. In the event we're not able to reach you within the
next couple of weeks, we have enclosed a remittance envelope
for your convenience.

*Figure 4-18. Solicitation letter used in connection with a phonothon
campaign (higher education)*

87

HANDICAPPED CHILDREN'S CENTER

It happens every year...

the people of Jacksonville respond generously to appeals for support from the Handicapped Children's Center.

Some give modest gifts, others large gifts. But most importantly, all seem to understand the Center's need for their help. Result: they do what they can.

My purpose in writing is to invite you to follow their example...to join with them in this vital, life-lifting work.

Your contribution will be gratefully received and acknowledged, and it will be used with maximum effectiveness to benefit the children involved.

Won't you take a moment now--this very day--to send in your contribution? A remittance envelope is enclosed for your convenience.

From all of us at the Center, and especially from the children, thanks!

Sincerely,

Harold Blakely

Harold "Ted" Blakely
Campaign Chairman

P. S. Our annual Open House will be held the week of July 11-15, from 10 to 3 each day. You and your family are cordially invited.

JACKSONVILLE

Figure 4-19. Solicitation letter (community service)

RICKS
COLLEGE

Dear Ricks Alumnus:

If you have a moment, I'd like to talk to you about money.
About $3, specifically. $3 isn't very much. If you're like
me, you'll spend more than that within a day or two on an
innocent indulgence.

But if you and the 28,333 other Ricks College alumni contributed $3 to your alma mater, you could establish an $85,000
endowment for the David O. McKay Library.

It's a $3 investment that might be the best you'll ever
make because you'll become a "shareholder" in one of the
finest libraries to be found on any U. S. junior college
campus. Moreover, your $3 will make an enduring contri-
bution to the education of over 5,000 deserving young men
and women who are at Ricks today and who will be here tomorrow.

Then, too, your $3 gift will give you the special satisfac-
tion that comes with knowing you've given meaningful
assistance to a meaningful institution of higher learning--
a place and a people worthy of your support.

$3--won't you make it available now simply by writing out
your check and returning it in the enclosed envelope?

Please know that we're grateful for all you do--in many
ways--to further the programs of Ricks. If we haven't said
so lately, let us say so now: we appreciate you.

Sincerely,

Dewain Silvester

Dewain Silvester, President

P.S. If you can give more than $3, we can use it.

Figure 4-20. Solicitation letter (higher education)

UTAH VALLEY HOSPITAL
1034 North 500 West / Provo, Utah 84601

Hospitals are for helping.

You know that. But sometimes before hospitals can help, they must be helped. That's the way it is right now for Utah Valley Hospital. UVH is in the middle of a $19 million expansion program that will benefit you and those you love for generations to come.

Specifically, the expansion will: * Increase floor space by 189,500 square feet. * Provide 203 new acute medical surgical patient beds, including a 24-bed intensive care unit. * Provide an expanded emergency center and 18 outpatient "holding beds." * Double the size of the radiology department and pharmacy. * Provide expanded parking.

The hospital's sponsor has arranged the bonding for most of the funding. $4 million, however, must come from other sources, including UVH employees and volunteers, medical staff, businesses, and individual citizens--people like you.

Your contribution is essential if we are to raise the $4 million.

How much should you give? That, of course, is your decision. You know your individual circumstances best, but we respectfully suggest a minimum gift of $25.

I hope that you will help...that you will look upon this appeal as an opportunity to invest in quality medical care for yourself and for those you love.

Please send in your contribution soon.

Thanks!

Sincerely,

Mark J. Howard

Mark J. Howard
Executive Secretary, Fund-Raising Committee

P. S. A postage-paid, pre-addressed remittance envelope is enclosed for your convenience.

Figure 4-21. Solicitation letter (health care)

5

MODEL APPROACHES TO INDIVIDUALS, FOUNDATIONS, AND CORPORATIONS

There are many different ways to approach the three fund-raising markets: individuals, foundations, and corporations. Almost every fund raiser has a favorite story about a far-out approach that worked. (These have been known to evoke some hysterical laughter at fund-raising conferences.) The intent here, however, is to focus on those select, high-percentage-return approaches that have the best chance of succeeding.

For the purposes of this chapter, let's assume that you are a successful, civic-minded citizen who has just accepted a request from the president of the Stevensville Boys' Club to help raise $30,000 to improve the clubhouse gymnasium.

You know that a broad-swath, mass appeal campaign is out. Such a campaign has already been conducted in Stevensville for the gymnasium project. It involved a phonothon, fund-raising projects by the boys (car washing, grass cutting), and a door-to-door campaign by club leaders and volunteers. Total yield: $12,700. The $30,000 you must raise is needed in *addition* to the $12,700.

The paragraphs that follow describe how you might best approach individuals, foundations, and corporations on behalf of the Stevensville Boys' Club — or any similar organization. In each instance it is assumed that you have completed the appropriate preliminary steps described in Chapter 3.

INDIVIDUALS

From your prospect file you should select six or seven individuals who seem promising, because of: 1) wealth, 2) interest in youth (sports, outdoor recreation, scouting, etc.), 3) past giving patterns, 4) tax situation, and 5) strong community ties.

Your first step is to talk with people who can give you current, reliable information about the prospects. When you approach them, be aboveboard about your intent: "Dr. Green, I'm considering asking Mr. Baird to make a large contribution to the Boys' Club. I need your help, though, in getting some information about him. Would you mind answering a few questions for me?" If Dr. Green declines, others will not, and eventually you'll be able to ask questions like these:

- Is Mr. Baird's financial condition still sound?

- I know he has some stock plus land on the beach, but are you aware of any other assets?

- He has supported the Boys' Club for several years with small gifts. Do you know if he has any other charitable interests?

- Has he ever said anything to you about how he intends to use his wealth?

- Can you give me the names of some of his other friends?

- Would you say that Mr. Baird has an average or above average need for social recognition?

After you have investigated the other prospects, let's say that Mr. Baird turns out to be the most promising. From Dr. Green and others you learn that Mrs. Baird is deceased, and that the couple's two children are both financially successful in their own right.

You also learn that Mr. Baird has spoken favorably about community programs to help the disadvantaged, especially young people. You make two important discoveries about his financial situation: 1) He recently sold some of his land and faces a stiff capital gains tax, and 2) he holds several hundred shares of stock purchased several years ago through an employee stock plan. You learn that Mr. Baird is about average in his need for social recognition, and you are told his best friend is Fred Driggs.

Visit with Fred Driggs for additional insights. Be careful to avoid any suggestion that you are inviting him to join with you in a "plot" involving his best friend. Mr. Driggs may be reserved in his responses, but he will likely verify the accuracy of your information — and add a fact or two. Do *not* ask him to keep your meeting confidential. It may be to your advantage to have him alert Mr. Baird to your intentions. (Actually, as discussed in Chapter 3, carefully letting the prospect know that you intend to ask for a gift is a necessary part of the cultivation process. If the prospect is totally surprised when you ask, your cultivation effort has fallen short.)

By now you have cleared all of the necessary hurdles, and the race begins in earnest. Call Mr. Baird and arrange an appointment with him. Lunch at his favorite restaurant (which Fred Driggs identified for you) is a good format. Your telephone conversation might go something like this:

> "Mr. Baird? My name is _____. I don't believe you know me. I'm working with the Stevensville Boys' Club on a fund-raising project. I know of your interest in young people and their problems, and I want very much to meet with you and discuss the Boys' Club building program. I think you'll find it interesting and worthwhile. Could we get together sometime soon at Bratton's — my schedule is open...what would work best for you?"

Give careful thought to whether or not someone besides you and Mr. Baird should attend the luncheon meeting. For example, if Mr. Baird is likely to make the gift in deferred form, such as a charitable remainder trust, you should seriously consider having an attorney attend. Realize, though, that involving an attorney might be perceived as presumptuous by Mr. Baird. Consequently, carefully weigh all the factors involved. Also consider the possibility of having someone else — an individual held in high esteem by Mr. Baird — present your case. Again, weigh the factors, then act. Whatever you decide, *spring no surprises on Mr. Baird.*

If you plan to go to the meeting without an attorney, consult with one to determine how Mr. Baird can best make the gift from a tax standpoint. (The attorney may well advise Mr. Baird to give the Boys' Club $30,000 worth of his stock. This approach will enable him to avoid paying capital gains tax for which he would be liable if he sold the stock — the situation he faces with the land sale. In addition, Mr. Baird will be able to claim a charitable tax deduction on his tax return, and reduce the amount of federal estate tax that will eventually come due on his property. As this example indicates, tax-planned giving is complex, so rely on legal counsel. Publications to help acquaint you with the subject are available.)

From discussions with the Boys' Club president and governing board, determine in advance of the luncheon whether or not they are prepared to erect a plaque at the gymnasium honoring Mr. Baird for his contribution. This question inevitably comes up, so be prepared for it.

At the meeting, use the in-person asking technique and the tools described in Chapter 4.

Mr. Baird will probably tell you one of three things: 1) "Yes, I will give the Stevensville Boys' Club $30,000"; 2) "I want to help the Boys' Club, but $30,000 is more than I want to give. I'll give you $_____"; 3) "No, I'm sorry, I am not in a position to help." If Mr. Baird responds with 1 or 2, implement the steps described in Chapter 6. If he responds with 2 or 3, do not move to the next market (foundations); rather, move to the next best individual prospect on your original list. Why? *Individuals* with strong local ties are the best of all possible prospects.

FOUNDATIONS

Foundations as a whole are something of an American mystery, so, first, some background. No one knows the exact wealth of foundations at any given moment, because their portfolios fatten and flatten with the vagaries of the economy and with changes in tax laws.

Dwight McDonald's definition of one particular foundation (Ford) is memorable: "...a large body of money completely surrounded by people who want some."[1]

But F. Emerson Andrews' definition is the most meaningful: ["A foundation is]...nongovernmental, nonprofit, has a principal fund of its own, is managed by its own trustees and directors, is established to maintain or aid social, educational, charitable, religious, or other activities serving the common welfare."[2]

Foundations, which are predominately an American phenomenon, take four basic forms in the United States. (The author is indebted to The Foundation Center for the information that follows.)

Independent. These are independent grantmaking entities established to promote educational, social, religious, or other charitable causes. Their endowments are generally derived from a single source (individuals, groups of individuals, or families). Grantmaking decisions may be made by the donor, donor's family, independent board of directors or trustees, or by a bank or trust officer acting on the donor's behalf. Many independent foundations give only in a few specific fields, and about 70 percent limit their giving to a local area.

Company-sponsored. These have close ties to the corporations that provide their funding (in the form of endowments and annual contributions), but they are legally independent. Some use their endowments to provide grants in years when corporate profits are down. Grantmaking decisions may or may not be made by associated corporate officials. Company-sponsored foundations tend to give in fields related to corporate activities or in communities in which the corporation has plants or other operations. Although they usually give a larger number of grants than independent foundations, the dollar amount involved in each grant tends to be smaller.

Operating. These use their resources to conduct research or to provide a direct service. Their endowment usually comes from a single source, and grantmaking decisions are made by an independent board of directors. They make few, if any grants, and then only when the project relates directly to the research they are conducting or to the service they are providing.

Community. These are publicly supported organizations that make grants for social, religious, educational, or other charitable purposes in a specific community or region. They receive contributions from many different donors (individual citizens, for example, who want to help their town). Grantmaking decisions are usually made by a board of directors representing a cross-section of the community. Grants made by community foundations are almost always limited to charitable organizations within the communities in which they operate.

For you as an American fund raiser, though, what matters most is that The Foundation Center (79 Fifth Avenue, 8th Floor, New York, NY 10003; phone 800-424-9836) publishes — every two years — an authoritative tome known as "The Foundation Directory," which describes thousands of foundations. These are the ones that merit your attention: They account for around 90 percent of the assets of foundations in the United States and for about 85 percent of the total grant dollars awarded by private foundations.

Without the Directory or its equivalent (several other good guides are available), you will find it difficult to raise foundation funds on behalf of the Stevensville Boys' Club — or any other organization. The Directory, available in many public libraries, offers a remarkable range of information about the nation's most active grantmaking foundations, including:

- Names, addresses, telephone numbers, and date and place of their founding.

- Who founded them and for what purpose, including a detailed description of their areas of interest ("...emphasis primarily on direct social services, particularly for the elderly and handicapped") and the geographical areas in which they give ("grants limited to California and Texas").

- Total assets; number of grants made and dollar value, including smallest and largest grants; names of officers, trustees, or directors.

- Whom to write to; and when and in what form to submit grant applications.

The Foundation Center provides other publications and services as well, including:

- A nationwide network of reference collections for free public use. Reference libraries in New York City, Washington, D.C., Cleveland, and San Francisco offer a wide variety of user services and comprehensive collections of foundation materials, including all Center publications; books, services, and periodicals on philanthropy; and foundation annual reports, newsletters, and press clippings. Cooperating collections, which are located in most states, contain complete collections of Foundation Center publications, as well as IRS records for foundations that operate in the state in which each collection is located.

- An annual subscription service called Source Book Profiles that provides a detailed description of the 1,000 largest foundations. Giving patterns are analyzed by subject area, type of support, and type of recipient. The service operates on a two-year publishing cycle, with each one-year series covering 500 foundations. Each quarterly installment includes about 125 new profiles as well as information on changes in address, telephone, personnel or program, and a revised, cumulative set of indexes.

- A guide to grants of $5,000 or more awarded to nonprofit organizations by about 450 major foundations in the United States. Known as the Foundation Grants Index Bimonthly, this publication also includes cumulative lists of annual reports and information brochures issued by foundations and corporate grantmakers; a calendar of events and seminars of interest to fund raisers; an update service listing changes in grantmakers' policy, priorities, personnel, etc.; and other helpful information.

- A series of computer-produced guides to foundation giving called COMSEARCH Printouts. The guides are issued in four separate categories: *COMSEARCH,*

Broad Topics, which lists all grants made by foundations in 17 broad subject categories during the previous year; *COMSEARCH, Subjects,* which presents 68 specially focused subject listings of grants made during the previous year, arranged by the state in which each grantmaking foundation is located; *COMSEARCH, Geographic,* which provides customized listings of grants received by organizations in two cities, eleven states, and four regions (the intent of this service is to help fund raisers identify the major foundations that have awarded grants in their areas); *COMSEARCH, Special Topics,* which lists the 1,000 largest foundations in the United States by assets and total giving, and the 1,300 operating foundations in the United States that administer their own projects or programs.

Now, back to the Stevensville Boys' Club. When you get your hands on "The Foundation Directory," turn to the Index of Fields of Interest at the back. The special interests of many of the foundations listed in the Directory proper appear there. At least six headings should draw your interest: Child Development, Child Welfare, Community Funds, Recreation, Social Services, and Youth. You will find references to a few hundred foundations under these six headings, and, as a result, you will have some excellent leads!

Give special attention to the Community Funds heading. Invariably, foundations with an interest in community funds are *company-sponsored foundations.* Because Stevensville is located near a corporation with a company-sponsored foundation, you are in an enviable position to approach that foundation. This is true for at least two reasons: 1) Company-sponsored foundations are unabashedly interested in building community goodwill for their founding firms, and 2) the firm's employees are likely to benefit directly from the proposed project.

Case in point: A hospital in a Utah community was seeking funds for a multimillion dollar expansion program. The management of a large corporation located nearby was interested in the hospital expansion, because it was seen as vital to adequate health care for their employees — and for a planned expansion of its own. Management also wanted to be a "good neighbor" in the community and suggested that the hospital's fund-raising director approach the foundation and ask for $1 million. He did, and he got it!

Let's assume now that you have identified, researched, and settled on at least one promising foundation prospect. In the process you have assured yourself of the following.

- Stevensville Boys' Club is within the foundation's area of interest.

- The foundation *does* support brick-and-mortar type projects. (Many foundations do not — they give only for research or programs.)

- The foundation is not prohibited by its charter from giving in your state or city.

- The amount of money you seek is within the foundation's customary giving range.

What next? Unfortunately, there is no simple answer to that question. In the author's view, however, it makes sense to establish a relationship with the foundation that goes beyond exchanging letters in the mail. This suggests a visit with an officer of the foundation. Although many foundation officers firmly declare that they give as much attention to proposals that arrive in the mail as they do to those that are brought to them in person, there is evidence to suggest otherwise. *People relate to people.* Consequently, it makes sense to phone or write the foundation and request an interview appointment. In seeking an appointment, couch your project in terms of the *foundation's* interests. ("This project, Mrs. _____, is consistent with your foundation's interests, concerns, and past patterns of philanthropic support.") Avoid anything controversial or hard sell. Drop names if you can do so legitimately. Better still, have someone who is well known to the foundation make the appointment.

If you are *not* granted an interview, you should still end up ahead — with valuable additional insights about your foundation prospect. Refusals are almost always delivered with some helpful words of illuminating explanation.

If you *are* granted an interview, go to it well prepared. If you are not thoroughly knowledgeable about project details, take along someone who is. Almost without exception, those closest to a project speak the most compellingly and convincingly for it (even if they seem to be nearly incoherent on other subjects!).

The purpose of the interview is about the same as the purpose of the opening round of a boxing match: to introduce the combatants and prepare them for the give and take that follows. For this reason, you usually don't ask for the grant in the interview, and you don't leave the written request. Instead, you listen, learn, and incorporate your new knowledge into the presentation to be made later.

Please understand, though, that the foundation has a right to expect something definite out of you — an innovative, exciting, well-thought-out idea of some kind, whether it's an improved gymnasium for a Boys' Club or a new approach to the problem of child abuse. You must show evidence of having done your homework. Your institution must come across as a place with some thoughtfully drawn plans as well as with the commitment, knowledge, and experience to bring them to fruition. Consequently, if the foundation perceives you as someone whose paramount interest is money rather than the power of money to implement constructive change, you will not make a positive impression. Foundations are not interested in hearing your problems. They *are* interested, however, in hearing *solutions* to your problems — solutions that will work for you *and for others.*

After the interview, it is unlikely that you will be invited back to make the presentation in person (the foundation officer's time is the problem). But if you are, keep it short, straightforward, and allow ample time for questions. Use simple, highly functional communication tools, such as the charts described in Chapter 4. Leave the written request, prepared in accordance with the outline given in Chapter 4 and tailored to reflect what you learned in the interview. Again, involve in the meeting those most knowledgeable about your project.

If you are not invited to make the presentation in person, submit your written request by mail with a cover letter. Make the letter warm but businesslike. Express appreciation for the interview, and address the letter to the person who interviewed you. Include a copy of your annual report if one is available.

A model cover letter is shown in Figure 5-1 at the end of this chapter.

Many foundations suggest that your first contact with them should be in the form of a one- or two-page "letter of inquiry." This advice is typically worded as follows: "Applicants are asked to send a letter to the foundation which includes a brief description of the project, what it is designed to do, and any other relevant background information. If the foundation is interested in receiving a full proposal, it will so advise the applicant." Presumably, an interview appointment and a chance to present your proposal would then follow.

You may, indeed, want to take this advice. On the other hand, if you use the request format described in Chapter 4, you have, in effect, the same thing as a "letter of inquiry" (the summary) plus some helpful backup information that may well have more persuasive power and impact than a letter alone could ever have. Part of the secret is to stand out from the crowd, and let's face it — it's tough to do that if you do exactly what everyone else does.

In case you're wondering if foundations provide application forms that you merely fill in and submit — much like applying for a government grant — the answer is, with some exceptions, no.

If you're applying to a large foundation, one of its officers will probably acknowledge receipt of your request within two weeks or so. If you are applying to a small-to-medium-sized foundation, especially if it does not have a full-time staff, you may never hear anything (really!). If more than a month goes by without any word, query the foundation by letter or phone.

Even if it looks like the Stevensville Boys' Club is going to receive a foundation grant, don't schedule a "gym warming" right away. Some foundations meet as infrequently as once a year to act on requests! Remember, too, that if you do receive a grant, it may not be for the full $30,000. Consequently, keep your options open.

Finally, a few words about foundations and direct mail. Let's assume that in your research you uncovered 30 or 40 foundations that seemed to be fairly good prospects — not outstanding, but worth a modest try. You can't afford to visit them in person, and you don't feel they merit a full-blown written request. The answer? Direct mail. Send them a simple folder or brochure and a cover letter. Some foundations will not respond to direct mail appeals, and they say so in "The Foundation Directory." But others will, and they are worth a try. One university sent out a mail appeal to nearly 200 foundations. Only one responded — with a $50,000 grant.

CORPORATIONS

Unlike foundations, corporations are not in business to give their money away. In fact, corporations are not at all charitable in the classical sense of the word. Charity requires that people give their *own* money away. When corporations give to charity, however, they are giving their *shareholders'* money away. Irving Kristol, writing in The Wall Street Journal, explains the special responsibility this entails: "When you give away your own money, you can be as foolish, as arbitrary, as whimsical as you like. But when you give away your stockholders' money, your philanthropy must serve the longer-term interests of the corporation. Corporate philanthropy should not be, cannot be disinterested."[3]

Little wonder then that corporate giving is heavily involved in "enlightened self-interest." Nevertheless, the scope of such giving is only a fraction of what it might be. Many companies give little or nothing, even though a survey of 600 chief executive officers by Mutual Benefit Life Insurance Company showed that 91 percent acknowledged a sense of philanthropic responsibility, with only 6 percent indicating no responsibility.[4]

What does all this mean for you and the Stevensville Boys' Club? Simply this: Corporations are not likely to be the most promising of your prospects. Approach them with your eyes wide open and concentrate on those that stand to gain by giving to you. That gain may involve public relations, community goodwill, helpful sales contacts — any number of solid, good-for-business factors.

Look around Stevensville. Pick out the six or seven biggest, most prosperous businesses. Read their annual reports. Study their organization charts. Learn the names and backgrounds of their top executives. Find out who handles their charitable requests. The president? Vice president? Committee? Corporate giving officer? Public relations director? (Big companies have special departments for this purpose. One oil company, for example, has a "manager of community development"; another, a "corporate contributions counselor.")

Review the companies' past giving patterns. You will find that some give only to higher education — on the theory that they are obligated to support the institutions that educate their work force. This support takes many forms, including research grants, scholarships and fellowships, endowment grants, and work-study programs. You will find that others: 1) make cash grants to worthy community projects; 2) give equipment and material assistance to a variety of institutions; and 3) make executives or specialists available to charitable organizations, on a full-time basis, for several months or more.

Zero in on two or three prime prospects by asking yourself the following questions.

- Will this company be able to consider its contribution as an investment that will return tangible dividends — community good will, improved employee morale, "good neighbor" image, positive publicity, etc.?

- Is the company at this moment in special need of a public relations "coup" because of labor unrest, a disquieting disclosure, environmental incident, recent reduction in force, etc.?

- Does my project align philosophically or materially with the products or services of this company? (If so, you should strongly consider approaching the company for a contribution of those services or products. For example, you might ask the Stevensville Brick Foundry to contribute bricks; Stevensville Plumbing, to contribute the plumbing work; Stevensville Roofing, the roof; etc.).

- Do this company's employees stand to benefit directly from the gymnasium? For example, will children of the workers be using the improved gym?

After you have identified your best corporate prospects, face up to this fact: It's highly unlikely that any one of them is going to give you $30,000. Few companies want to set that kind of precedent, because it would open them up to other organizations' requests that they could not honor. (In the case of a public company, there's also the matter of stockholder relations.) For these reasons, you must assign a *realistic* quota to each company. Firm quota guidelines are not likely to be reliable, so you must consider the individual circumstances of each company. Is it sound? Are its prospects bright? Does it have strong local ties? Has it demonstrated a sense of "corporate citizenship" in the past? If it has given to community projects, how much did it give? Is its top management friendly to the Boys' Club? Whatever figure you arrive at, it probably shouldn't be more than $10,000. Again, though, individual circumstances must dictate.

Use the in-person asking technique and tools. As in the case of foundations, take along those who can best speak for your cause. Also, try to involve at least one influential member of the community in your presentation. Don't be bashful about revealing what other companies in the community are doing, especially if they are competitors and their gifts are good ones. Quite often, for example, a bank giving officer will not commit to a specific amount until he or she knows what other banks are giving. For this reason, go first to your very best prospects within a given business field and try to get them to make precedent-setting gifts.

The post-asking suggestions in Chapter 6 relate primarily to individuals. Some, however, are adaptable to corporations. Apply them as appropriate.

For relatively small companies and those that are not prime prospects, here are two other possibilities: 1) A door-to-door campaign involving an adult volunteer and one of the boys, and 2) direct mail. If you use the latter, make your appeal as personal as possible. Since you will not be mailing to a large number of companies, individually type and personalize each letter. Keep the

mailer simple so that you can hold down production costs (otherwise, you run the risk of not recovering your investment, to say nothing of failing to make a "profit").

Notes

1. Merrimon Cuninggim, "Private Money and Public Service" (New York: McGraw-Hill Book Company, 1972), p. 137.
2. Warren Weaver, "U.S. Philanthropic Foundations" (New York: Harper and Row, 1967), p. 39.
3. Wall Street Journal, March 21, 1977.
4. "Giving USA, 1984 Annual Report" (New York: American Association of Fund-Raising Counsel, Inc., 1984), p. 36.

BOYS'CLUB OF UTAH COUNTY

Mr.
Chairman of the Board
Foundation
P. O. Box 1.7.
en , Nevada 9

Dear Mr. Bergen:

President Crandall and I enjoyed the opportunity to meet
with you last week to discuss plans for our new club house.
It was kind of you to take the time to see us.

I am pleased to enclose our proposal to the
Foundation for a $50,000 grant to the Utah County Boys'
Club to assist with construction of the club house.

My associates and I sincerely believe that such a grant
would be a sound investment in our community, benefiting
hundreds of young men for generations to come.

We hope that you will give our proposal careful, thoughtful consideration.

If I can help by answering questions you may have, making
arrangements for you to visit the construction site, or
in some other way, please call on me.

Thank you again for your interest and concern.

Very truly yours,

Alan R. Robinson
Executive Director

Figure 5-1. Cover letter for request to foundation

6

AFTER YOU ASK

Whether your prospect's answer is "yes" or "no," your job isn't over once you've asked. In fact, it's just begun! This chapter describes the important steps you should take after you get your answer.

IF THE ANSWER IS 'YES'

Obviously, the first thing you should do is to express your appreciation to the donor. But how is that best done? A telephone call? Letter? Personal visit?

The answer depends on the amount of money the donor has contributed. Although a small thank-you can be every bit as sincere and meaningful as a large thank-you, it ultimately comes down to what is appropriate. Large gifts require more than simple expressions of appreciation — both recipient and donor usually recognize this fact.

The paragraphs that follow will present thank-you guidelines for four levels of giving: $100,000 and up, $25,000 to $100,000, $10,000 to $25,000 (defined here as the "upper levels" of giving) and $1 to $10,000 (defined here as the "lower level" of giving). These guidelines not only give you a blueprint for appropriate action, they also help to ensure that Donor Y who gives you $15,000 receives about the same treatment as Donor Z who gives you $15,000. Remember that they are only guidelines, and that you should adapt them as individual circumstances dictate.

Remember, too, that you should record, receipt, and acknowledge *every* gift, regardless of its size. You should do so to promote sound fund-raising management, accurate reporting (for internal and governmental purposes), and authentic tax documentation for your donors. The combined Thank You/This Is Your Receipt form (Figure 6-1 at the end of this chapter) is an efficient, economical way to accomplish all three functions. Prepare the form in duplicate so that you will have a copy for your files. Note that the form shown in Figure 6-1 makes a point of the fact that individual acknowledgment of every gift is prohibitively expensive, so "we hope you will accept this communication as a simple but sincere expression of our gratitude." This statement is aimed, of course, at those donors whose gifts are modest and who will not receive a personalized acknowledgment.

Fund raisers sometimes puzzle over how much to spend on thank-you activities. National practice suggests 1½ percent to 3 percent of the contribution. For example, a $10,000 gift would suggest a $150 to $300 expenditure.

$100,000 and up. Assume that Mr. L. W. Bird has given your institution $200,000 to establish a scholarship fund. Clearly, a letter or telephone call is an inappropriate way to say thanks. Mr. Bird should receive a visit — by appointment — from the president, director, or chief executive of your institution (hereafter "president") and key officers. They should take that opportunity to thank Mr. Bird in a warm, sincere, enthusiastic way. They should look him in the eye, shake his hand, and make no bones about how pleased they are. (If Mr. Bird lives several hundred miles away, then a visit by a representative of your institution who lives in the area would be appropriate. He should personally present a letter from your president to Mr. Bird. If Mr. Bird is not available for a personal visit within a month after the gift is received, then a letter from the president should be sent. It should, however, be followed by a personal visit as soon as circumstances permit.)

Mr. Bird should be told that your institution wants to honor him at a luncheon, dinner, faculty meeting, or in some other appropriate fashion. Ideas should be presented to Mr. Bird for his consideration, then adapted to conform with his wishes. Some donors are uncomfortable in the limelight. Consequently, you should be prepared to opt for a small, quiet get-together for lunch or dinner. Others will feel differently, and will forthrightly tell you so. Some will present you with a 500-name guest list for an announcement and appreciation banquet at the Hotel Ritz ballroom to be attended by your state's entire congressional delegation! If you're smart, you'll smile and tell them you think that's a marvelous idea. Then you'll set to work to make it a truly memorable event.

If donors do decide on some kind of public event, you must work closely with them or their representatives to see that their wishes are met. Questions to be resolved include the following: Who is to be invited? Who is to speak? Where is the event to be held? Is the gift to be announced at the event or before the event? (If the former approach is taken, are news media representatives to be invited?)

The event should include distribution of a booklet commemorating the donor's gift. The booklet should include a brief biography and photographs of the donor (family album photos showing the donor and his or her family through the years are excellent), and an explanation of how the gift will benefit those served by your institution. Such bookets are not only effective in paying tribute to the donor, they are also effective as cultivational literature to encourage other prospects to make similar gifts. Representative cover, page layout, and paragraphs from such booklets that have been nationally recognized for excellence are presented in Figures 6-2, 6-3, and 6-4 at the end of this chapter.

Within a week after the event has been held, the president should send Mr. Bird a letter that again thanks him for his gift, refers to favorable comments that have been received, and sets the tone for a mutually rewarding future relationship. A suggested letter is shown in Figure 6-5. Ideally, the form in Figure 6-1 should not be sent to donors at the upper giving levels until this letter and the other personalized thank-you procedures have been completed.

If all of this seems like a lot of trouble, ask yourself how long it would take you and your staff to earn the $200,000 that Mr. Bird contributed to your institution, the thousands of additional dollars that he may contribute in the future, and the thousands of other dollars that may be contributed by others stimulated by Mr. Bird's example.

Avoid the time-worn practice of awarding plaques, desk sets, paperweights, and similar off-the-shelf items to donors at the upper giving levels. These are not likely to make a good impression. Try, instead, to select unique gifts tailored to each donor's background and interests. One university, for example, gave a Navajo-made quartz chess set to a donor who had established a scholarship fund for American Indian students. And a hospital administrator whose institution had received a large cash donation from a broadcasting executive gave the donor an antique radio. A brass plate affixed to it carried an appropriate inscription.

$25,000 to $100,000. At this level, too, a personal visit is entirely appropriate, although a presidential letter will probably suffice. You should remember, however, that some donors will contribute relatively modest amounts initially to an institution to see how well they are received. If the reaction is a positive and appreciative one, they give additional gifts in larger amounts. Frankly, under such circumstances, a personal visit, in addition to being a thoughtful gesture, may well be an excellent investment.

Luncheons, dinners, or other special events honoring donors at this level are proper; however, they should not be large affairs. The rule here is quality on a small scale. A dinner at a fine restaurant involving the president, one or two other executives, and the donor and his or her family would be entirely in order. Many donors are justifiably put off when institutions spend lavishly on frills. Institutions that do so may unwittingly demonstrate that they are financially irresponsible. That, of course, is the one message you don't want your donors to get.

Here, too, a warm letter that sets the tone for a good future relationship is appropriate about a week or so after the thank-you event is held (Figure 6-5 at the end of this chapter).

Some donors who give at this level — and, indeed, at other levels as well — will tend to feel they "own" your institution. A small minority will attempt to capitalize on your sense of obligation to them by demanding certain privileges, special treatment, and other trappings of power and influence. If you are too eager in responding to these demands, you may be inviting still other demands. Consequently, it is important to establish a written policy stating what you are and are not willing to do to accommodate donors beyond the initial thank-you event. The development offices of some colleges and universities, for example, routinely purchase block seating at football and basketball games for donors and prospective donors. This is a reasonable service that most institutions can comfortably provide. To attempt to provide certain other kinds of services, however, might clearly be inappropriate. Case in point: One donor asked to have use of a university's ballroom one night a month throughout the school year. Quite properly, his request was denied.

$10,000 to $25,000. For moderate to large fund-raising organizations (those raising $1 million or more annually), this is probably the lowest giving level that merits special treatment. The donor should receive a letter of thanks from the president and an invitation to lunch or some other low-key get-together.

Don't overlook on-site opportunities to inform donors better about your work and to entertain and involve them. A doctor at one hospital, for example, demonstrated an exciting diagnostic tool to a donor — a brain-scanning machine. The donor was so impressed that he gave a follow-up gift of several thousand dollars to purchase needed accessories for the scanner.

You can involve donors at the upper giving levels in many mutually rewarding ways. Almost without exception, donors who can afford to give at these levels have something worthwhile to say — about their business, about the economy, about values, about lessons they have learned. Many institutions — especially those in higher education — wisely involve these people in guest lectureships, panel discussions, demonstrations, committee assignments (including chairmanships), and in other service-oriented capacities. Be careful, of course, about asking donors to serve in ways that would give them unwarranted control over their own financial contributions.

$1 to $10,000. How you thank donors at this level depends on the size of your organization and its relationship with them. Many large fund-raising organizations do not give special acknowledgement (such as a presidential letter) for gifts of under $5,000. However, for some organizations, a gift of $5,000 or even $2,000 is a major windfall — perhaps the biggest they will ever receive.

Consequently, if the gift is a big one for *your* organization, thank the donor in the way that seems most appropriate. That may mean a personal visit, it may mean lunch or dinner, it may mean a presidential letter, and it may mean all three.

Donors at this level who give to moderate-to-large fund-raising organizations should not, in most cases, receive more than the Thank You/This Is Your Receipt form (Figure 6-1). There are two exceptions, however.

The first exception involves gifts, donors, or causes that are unique and worthy of special recognition. For example, the president of a college in a small town was greeted one afternoon by 20 high school students who gave him a bank bag containing $627 in cash. The students explained that the money was for the library addition the college was struggling to build. Since they planned to enroll soon at the college and use the library, the students wanted to do their part. Clearly, such a gift merits special recognition — perhaps a news story in the local paper plus lunch with the president and library director.

The second exception involves gift clubs. Membership in such clubs is awarded to donors who give at certain established levels, usually on an annual basis. For example, at a typical college a donor becomes a member of the Old Main Society with an annual contribution of $200; a member of the President's Club for an annual contribution of $500; and a lifetime member of the President's Club for a one-time contribution of $8,000. Membership is usually awarded automatically — not as a result of a specific request by the donor. Benefits of club membership typically include an annual banquet, quarterly newsletter, and plaque or certificate. One of the most important benefits, however, is the satisfaction donors derive from associating with a recognized, respected group. The "benefits" offered by gift clubs are, in reality, thank-you events. Make certain that you follow through with them, so that your donors receive what you promised in your initial membership announcement.

Some fund raisers justify a relatively high thank-you expenditure for gift clubs — say 5 percent or 10 percent above regular fund-raising overhead — on the ground that special expressions of appreciation will bear fruit later in the form of larger contributions and, eventually, bequests. You may also be inclined to use this rationale. Remember, however, that the credibility of your entire program can be negatively affected by overspending on thank-you events that are, after all, highly visible and therefore especially susceptible to public disenchantment.

Other post-gift guidelines. Because past donors are your best prospects for future gifts, you should do more than thank them. You should initiate and maintain an ongoing cultivation program for them.

Donors at the higher giving levels should receive invitations to events in their areas of interest. At the beginning of each school year, for example, one large university sends donors interested in drama an announcement of plays scheduled for that year. The donors are asked to check the plays they would like to attend, and tickets are sent to them at the appropriate time. Another university keeps a file on donors with engineering backgrounds and involves them extensively in activities held during its annual engineering week.

It's also a good idea to put upper-level donors on distribution lists for publications and other materials in which they could be expected to have an interest. In fact, some institutions produce newsletters, magazines, and special reports expressly for donor cultivation. Typically, these publications report projects in progress, successes to date, and what could be accomplished if additional funding were available.

Large file cards containing data that will facilitate the cultivation of past donors are extremely helpful. Such cards should be prepared and maintained for all donors at the upper three giving levels. A suggested format is shown in Figure 6-6 at the end of this chapter. You may, of course, wish to consider putting such information on a computerized file and automating the whole process.

The names of donors at the lower giving level who consistently say "yes" to direct mail or other mass appeals should be placed in a "preferred donor" file and solicited differently than the others. This is important for two reasons.

First, because they are loyal givers, there is no reason for you to spend time and money on multiple contacts. One contact a year — a reminder — is usually all they need. You should, however, inform them of this fact: Tell them that because they have established themselves as loyal supporters, you will contact them only once a year (or at least less than you have been doing). Most will appreciate the fact that this approach reduces your overhead and increases the effectiveness of their contribution. A letter to announce and explain this approach is shown in Figure 6-7.

This technique is most applicable if your fund-raising program is run on a "campaign" basis — if you expect only, say, one gift a year from each donor to your annual giving campaign. Colleges typically structure their fund-raising campaigns in this manner.

However, other types of causes do not work on a campaign basis; they ask donors for gifts several times a year. (Some even send the donor a request for a new gift along *with* the acknowledgment of his or her current gift.) Causes like these typically do most of their fund raising by mail. And they find that they earn the best return on their fund-raising dollar when they approach their best donors for gifts *very* frequently. Good donors are good investments, they feel. With donors who give less frequently or who give smaller gifts, they invest fewer fund-raising dollars by mailing requests to them less frequently. So if you use a system like this, you also must segment your better donors out of your list.

Second, such a file will make it easy for you to identify donors who are good prospects for larger gifts, including membership in gift clubs such as a president's or director's club. Fund raisers at a large Midwestern university noticed, for example, in reviewing their "preferred donor" file, that one alumna had been contributing consistently for many years, and that her contributions were large. They researched the woman's background and not only discovered that she had substantial wealth, but also that she had a retarded child. They arranged to meet with her, and the eventual result was a $300,000 contribution to the university's center for learning-disabled children.

IF THE ANSWER IS 'NO'

If your prospect says "no," the worst thing you can do is to give up. By all means, try again — preferably within six months. Timing is critical to the success of charitable requests, especially those at the upper giving levels. Just because prospects turn you down today doesn't mean that they will turn you down six months from now. Their stock may be down. They may have just made a gift to another charitable institution. Their liquid assets may be at a premium at the moment. They may wish to check you out before they make any kind of commitment. There are many reasons why prospects say no, and very few of them are not susceptible to change.

The more you ask a given prospect, the better your chances of success. Most prospects find it difficult, even embarrassing, to say no more than three or four times, especially if the same person does the asking each time.

You should maintain a file card on all upper-level individuals you ask, whether you are asking them as individuals or as representatives of a company or foundation. The card should list the date they were asked, amount requested, who did the asking, and the prospect's response. Without such a card, you have no sure guide for follow-up action.

Is there ever a time when you should give up on prospects? Yes — when they tell you firmly that they aren't interested or request that you not contact them further.

Two years or more of "no" responses from individuals at the lower giving levels solicited by direct mail, in phonothons, or in other mass appeals suggests that you should give them a low solicitation priority. Specifically, you should contact them less often and devote less time and money to them. For example, if you are soliciting individuals at the lower giving levels three times a year by direct mail, you should consider contacting your "no" people only once a year — with a message tailored specifically to them. An example of one such message — a letter of proven effectiveness — is shown in Figure 6-8 at the end of this chapter.

Individuals at the lower giving levels who do not respond positively after three or four years of solicitation, should be eliminated from your list. They are a luxury you cannot afford. Money you spend soliciting them can be better spent identifying, researching, and soliciting new prospects.

Thanks! This is Your Receipt.

We really mean it. That "we" stands for many people you may never meet but who need and appreciate your financial support . . . people touched by Church education and health service programs worldwide. Because personalized acknowledgment of every gift is prohibitively expensive, we are not always able to send individual letters of appreciation. Consequently, we hope you will accept this communication as a simple but sincere expression of our gratitude.

Account Name

Account Number   Date   Donation Description

Barry B. Preator
Financial Accounting
The Development Office
P.O. Box 7188
University Station
Provo, Utah 84602

Gifts to charitable institutions are deductible for tax purposes under Sec. 170 of the IRS Code.

Figure 6-1. Combined "thank-you" and receipt form

Figure 6-2. Commemorative brochure — representative cover

Mr. Clyde's devotion to Scouting is reflected in the many improvements he made at the Maple Dell Scout Camp in Payson, which included this modern lodge.

Section of interstate near Salt Lake City under construction.

affairs, Mr. Clyde served as mayor of Springville; member, University of Utah Board of Regents and Utah Valley Industrial Development Association; and president, Associated General Contractors, Springville Chamber of Commerce, Springville Kiwanis Club, Springville Art Association, and Timpanogos Knife and Fork Club.

Long a leader in the Boy Scouts of America, he was president of the Utah National Parks Council for twelve years and held the Silver Beaver and Silver Antelope awards. While he was president,

the Scout Office Building in Provo was constructed and the following improvements were made at Maple Dell Scout Camp: swimming pool, amphitheater, and facilities for caretakers and Scout leaders. In addition, Mr. & Mrs. Clyde contributed a modern lodge to the camp.

He served as bishop of the Springville LDS Ninth Ward and as a member of the Springville Stake High Council.

Mr. Clyde's life of distinguished service and contributions was recognized with numerous awards: The BYU Jesse Knight

Figure 6-3. Commemorative brochure — representative page layout

*H*e that can heroically endure
adversity will bear prosper-
ity with equal greatness of soul;
for the mind that cannot
be dejected by the former is not likely
to be transported with the latter.
— Henry Fielding
  English novelist

INSTITUTE

Years from now, October 12, 19° 6 will be looked upon as an important date not only in the history of this institution, but in the history of business in American higher education.

It will be remembered as the beginning of the Skaggs Institute of Retail Management at Brigham Young University, established with a generous grant from the Skaggs Foundation.

Those who look back will see that the institute's inception signalled the start of a unique and nationally known organization — one expressly designed to provide academic *and* practical retailing education.

Proud statements? Perhaps. But people close to the institute believe in them. The information that follows — about the institute proper and the company that founded it — helps to reveal why.

To an extraordinary degree, Dr. and Mrs. Harold Merkley are Fielding's kind of people.

Adversity? They have known it — from the arduous, debt-ridden struggle through undergraduate and medical school, to the day-and-night toil of one-man doctoring in an isolated mining county of 5,000, to the bone-wearying work of starting a practice from scratch.

Mr. & Mrs. Clyde have made substantial philanthropic gifts to educational, scientific, religious, and cultural institutions, including Brigham Young University, the University of Utah, Utah State University, and — as mentioned earlier — the Boy Scouts of America.

In addition, through the Clyde Foundation (founded in 1962), Mr. & Mrs. Clyde were instrumental in the construction of the Clyde Memorial Galleries for the Springville Art Museum. The two-story wing, completed in 1964, is named in memory of Mr. Clyde's parents.

In the summer of 1914, Roland Rich Woolley, then twenty-three, borrowed $100 from a former missionary companion so he could travel to Washington, D. C., find a job, and enroll in law school. That loan launched Mr. Woolley on a distinguished legal career — a fact he hasn't forgotten. On April 13, 1973 he gave Brigham Young University $500,000 to establish a loan fund at the J. Reuben Clark Law School.

Figure 6-4. Commemorative brochure — representative paragraphs from several brochures

Castledale College
Wendover, Utah 84083

Mr. L. W. . J.
2. An.e. . Circle
Lincoln, Nebraska 685

Dear Mr. . i .:

The events of the past week have been a source of great
satisfaction to all of us here at the College.

We were delighted to have you and Mrs. i . as our guests
at dinner Friday evening. It was a special pleasure for us
to meet your many friends, including Senator and Mrs. .il.

Many people have commented about your generosity and
thoughtfulness in establishing the scholarship fund. Mayor
Hawkins told me he could think of no finer gift to the young
people of our community, and Mr. Lambert said the fund was
"one of the best ideas anyone has had to help our community
in many, many years."

May I take this opportunity to thank you again, Mr. i._,
for your contribution to our institution and its young
people.

We will, of course, provide you with a semi-annual report
on the fund. We will also arrange for you to meet with
students who will be benefitting from the fund. Quarterly
luncheons are planned for this purpose. If we can be of
service in some other way, please call on us.

Sincerely,

Brandon R. Ralphs

Brandon R. Ralphs, President

Figure 6-5. Letter to be sent following thank-you event

DONOR CULTIVATION DATA CARD Name _____ Age _____ Date _____

Address _____ City _____ State _____ Zip _____ Phone ( ) _____

Birth Date _____ Spouse's Name/Birth Date _____

Children's Names _____

Donor's Occupation _____ Giving History (gifts, value, when given) _____

Names of Close Friends/Business Associates _____

Interests/Hobbies/Accomplishments _____

List key factors that led donor to give to our organization _____

Religion _____ Political Pref. _____

Is Donor Favorable Toward Publicity? _____ Special Qualities, Needs, Problems
Relating to Donor _____

Describe here and on backside specific cultivation plan for future gifts, including publications, invitations to be extended, etc. _____

_____

Figure 6-6. Donor cultivation data card

The Development Office

Brigham Young University

Dear Friend of BYU:

Year in and year out you've been somebody we could count on--a steady supporter of Brigham Young University. If we haven't said so lately, let us say so now: we appreciate you!

My reason for writing is to ask your help in making our Annual Giving program as efficient as possible. Let me explain.

As you know, each year we depend on hundreds of volunteer workers to make personal contacts on behalf of BYU. If we could persuade you and the many others who contribute to BYU to make your contribution automatic, it would free our workers to zero in on those who have not yet demonstrated the loyalty you have.

What we propose to do is to simply remind you each year (via a computerized statement) of the need for your gift to BYU. The date the statement is mailed and the amount to be given are, of course, up to you. We call our program Auto Giving.

We hope we aren't being presumptuous, and we hope you can appreciate the time and money-saving advantages of an automatic statement program.

To initiate Auto Giving, fill in the enclosed card and return it in the pre-addressed envelope.

Thanks!

Sincerely,

Ken "J" Taylor, Assistant Director

P. S. Please respond by July 1.

University Station, P.O. Box 7188, Brigham Young University, Provo, Utah 84602
(801) 374-1211, Extension 4444

Figure 6-7. Letter to loyal givers announcing streamlined solicitation approach

Dallin H. Oaks
President

Brigham Young University

Talk to alumni who haven't contributed to BYU in the past
and you'll hear comments like this:

"I haven't given because, well, I haven't felt the University
really needed my money."

I want you to know that Brigham Young University does need
your financial support, and that your gift--large or small--
is welcomed and wanted.

We have innumerable needs as we begin our second century
of educational service--needs involving scholarships, loan
funds, research, endowed professorial chairs, and much more.

Many individuals--parents, friends, alumni--who have not
given to BYU in the past, have taken the opportunity to do
so in this first year of our second century.

I hope you will do the same.

Sincerely,

Dallin H. Oaks

D-346 ASB, Brigham Young University, Provo, Utah 84602 (801) 374-1211, Extension 2521

Figure 6-8. Letter to non-givers

7 ![ERI logo]   HOW IT HAPPENS: THREE CASE HISTORIES

If fund raisers kept diaries (some do), and if they were given to writing fiction (some are), a typical entry might read as follows.

"Dear Diary: What an incredible day! Just as I sat down at my desk this morning, Mr. B. J. Glassman called me. Yep, that's right — *the* Mr. Glassman. Imagine — *him* calling me...called all the way from Monaco. Oh, we had jokingly brought up his name a few times in our Prospect Consideration Meetings — along with those of John D. Rockefeller, Andrew Carnegie, and Henry Ford! But you know, he acted like he was my long-lost friend. Said he knew all about Oakville Hospital and our plans to add a 100-bed wing and the new emergency center. Said he thought it was the right thing to do, and — can you believe it? — said he wanted to help! Next thing I know he's asking me how much the whole thing will cost. I managed to mumble, 'Ah, ah, about $8 million, Mr. Glassman — that's with the automatic doors on the emergency center and all.' Then he said, 'Well, sir, would a million in a day or two and a million each month for the next seven months be OK? I mean cash, of course.' I'm almost choking by now, but I worry about sounding too eager (and besides that, I'm wondering if someone is playing a practical joke on me), so I come back with 'Well...hmmmm...we could probably accept that — yes, yes, I believe that would work out, Mr. Glassman. Ya, I definitely feel that it would...I think I have authority to say that.' Then he said, 'Fine, good, wonderful. I was hoping you would feel that way. Let's see now, what is the hospital's full legal name — so I get it on the checks correctly. Also, I need your ZIP code out there...' "

The foregoing is, of course, the wildest kind of fantasy. Anyone who has been raising funds for even a week knows that the chances of something like that happening are too remote to calculate. True, you do get some pleasant surprises every once in a while — a $100 bill in the mail from an anonymous donor with a note reading "keep up the great work"; an honest-in-heart prospect who comes knocking on *your* door; an envelope from a law firm containing notice of a $5,000 bequest to your organization. But almost without exception, truly substantial gifts involve months, sometimes years of painstaking planning, cultivation, and even negotiation. In short, most big gifts "happen" because able and ambitious fund-raisers *make* them happen.

The paragraphs that follow present three case histories of large gifts actually received by charitable organizations from individual donors. These histories are recommended reading because they dramatize the application of fund-raising principles that *work.* They have worked in the past for others and will work in the future for you. As you read the histories, look for evidence that the fund raisers have tried to:

- Establish a functional, efficient organization in which each worker's duties are clearly defined.

- Establish a just cause and effectively communicate it.

- Identify individuals who could reasonably be expected to contribute, and carefully evaluate their giving interests and potential.

- Cultivate prospects by honestly earning their friendship and trust.

- Apply, where appropriate, those factors that motivate people to give.

- Demonstrate personal commitment to their causes.

- Use existing facilities, services, special circumstances, and personnel (including volunteers) with maximum effectiveness.

- Involve appropriate people in cultivational and asking activities.

- Understand and capitalize on the *prospect's* value system, priorities, and frame of reference.

- Persevere, whatever the difficulties and setbacks.

- Make effective and optimum use of solicitation techniques and tools.

- Involve professionals when appropriate.

- Apply pressure to overcome prospect inertia.

- Tailor their requests to their prospects.

- Comply with ethical, professional standards of conduct.

The tax implications of making the various kinds of gifts described next are based on provisions of the various tax laws. Because new tax legislation is enacted with increasing frequency, it is essential for fund raisers to avail themselves of the most current information available, and to rely on professional legal counsel.

So the author could write freely about the events that took place, the names of the people involved in each case history are fictitious and the receiving organizations are not specifically identified.

CASE HISTORY A

Mrs. Brown, a wealthy, 63-year-old widow living in Nevada, read a wire service story describing encouraging progress a university speech researcher in California was making in treating stammering. Mrs. Brown's late husband had struggled with the handicap for years, and had made only marginal progress in overcoming it.

The story had been written by the university news director at the urging of Mr. Johnson, the university development director. The story contained a quote by the researcher, Dr. Glenn, in which he said, "With additional funding support, we can continue to make important progress in helping people with this difficult problem."

A few days after she had read the article, Mrs. Brown reached Dr. Glenn by phone at the university and asked several questions about his work. He was alert enough to sense that she was seriously interested in his research and a possible source of financial support. Dr. Glenn was courteous, helpful, and patient. He told Mrs. Brown he would like to send her some articles he had published, and asked for her name and address. She complied.

Dr. Glenn mailed the material to Mrs. Brown three days later, together with a warm, friendly cover letter. About two weeks after that, he received a simple thank-you note from Mrs. Brown. Dr. Glenn then went to Mr. Johnson (the development director) and told him about Mrs. Brown. Mr. Johnson asked Dr. Glenn to inform him of any future calls or letters from Mrs. Brown, and then asked his research supervisor (Mrs. Henderson) to find out all she could about Mrs. Brown and to give him a report.

Mrs. Henderson called an alumnus, Mr. Phillips, who lived in Mrs. Brown's city. Mr. Phillips was an attorney who had helped the university in various professional and volunteer capacities. Because Mrs. Brown's late husband had been a prominent CPA in the city, Mr. Phillips quickly was able to gather important information about the couple. Mr. Phillips talked to neighbors and former business associates of Mr. Brown, and located his obituary at the city library. Within a month, Mrs. Henderson had a substantial file on the Browns, including religious preference, political affiliation, value of the estate, past giving patterns, and organizational memberships.

Although Dr. Glenn had heard nothing further from Mrs. Brown, Mr. Johnson decided — on the basis of Mrs. Henderson's encouraging findings — to initiate a cultivation program. He asked Dr. Glenn to begin sending Mrs. Brown informative, nontechnical materials relating to speech therapy and communicative disorders. Each mailing was to be accompanied by a friendly, low-key, "thought you might be interested" cover letter signed by Dr. Glenn. Each cover letter was to include an invitation to call or write for additional information. Mr. Johnson asked his communications supervisor to help Dr. Glenn prepare the mailings.

After two mailings had been made (about one month's time), Mr. Johnson called Mr. Phillips (the volunteer-attorney) and asked him to invite Mrs. Brown and a companion to a play to be put on by the university's traveling drama group in Mrs. Brown's city.

Mr. Phillips was to explain that he was a friend of the university and of Dr. Glenn, and that he had been asked by Dr. Glenn to invite her to the play. Mrs. Brown accepted, and decided to attend the play with her daughter. Mr. Phillips picked them up at their home, took them to the play and then to dinner.

Over dessert, Mr. Phillips *carefully* talked about the university, Dr. Glenn's work, and the fact that people can sometimes help worthy causes — and themselves — through proper estate planning. He suggested that Mrs. Brown consider visiting the university and seeing at first hand the work of Dr. Glenn. Mrs. Brown was polite and attentive but noncommittal.

About a week later, Dr. Glenn called Mrs. Brown and invited her to be the university's guest for three days. Her visit would include a tour of Dr. Glenn's department, a visit with the university president, and a front-row seat at a concert. Mrs. Brown declined the offer. She gave no reason.

Dr. Glenn continued to send materials to her. In addition, Mr. Phillips began sending her commercially prepared pamphlets about the importance of wills and estate planning.

Several months passed. Dr. Glenn was preparing a regional-level workshop for speech therapists. Leading authorities from several states would be in attendance, and important papers would be presented. He decided that the workshop was an ideal excuse to invite Mrs. Brown again to the campus. Dr. Glenn wrote her a letter describing the workshop and inviting her to be the university's guest. He followed up the letter with a telephone call about a week later. This time Mrs. Brown accepted the invitation.

Mr. Johnson, his staff, and Dr. Glenn worked together to make certain that Mrs. Brown's visit was a *total* success. Some specifics:

- They met her at the airport and drove her to her hotel — one of the city's best.

- In her room, she found a basket of fruit with a card inscribed, "We hope your visit is enjoyable and memorable. Please call if there's anything you need. Dr. Glenn and _____ University.''

- They arranged for her to meet the university president, tour the campus (via electric golf cart), talk with students and patients in the speech therapy department, and visit several points of interest in the city and surrounding area. The president gave her an inscribed copy of a book he had just published.

- They *sincerely* sought her comments and suggestions about higher education in general and about speech problems in particular.

- When it was time for her to leave, they dropped by the president's office. He thanked her for coming and wished her an enjoyable trip home. Then they drove her to the airport.

A few days after Mrs. Brown's departure, Dr. Glenn sent a brief note thanking her for her visit. Included with the note were copies of some of the papers presented at the workshop.

About two weeks later, Mr. Phillips called Mrs. Brown and told her that he and Dr. Glenn would like to meet with her in her home to discuss some ways in which she could further Dr. Glenn's work and possibly strengthen her financial position. Mrs. Brown agreed to meet them.

Before Mr. Phillips and Dr. Glenn visited Mrs. Brown and asked for the gift, Mr. Phillips determined how much to ask for and what form the gift should take. These decisions were based on the best available information about Mrs. Brown's assets.

Outcome. Mrs. Brown decided to place her $500,000 estate in a short-term trust with the university, restricted to Glenn's department. Upon her death, the university will receive annually a specified percentage of the initial value of the trust for 10 years. After this period, the trust will end and the daughter will own the property. This arrangement will probably eliminate the estate tax on Mrs. Brown's estate.

CASE HISTORY B

A private, church-sponsored college in the Midwest had been cultivating the 60-ish owner of a chain of restaurants (Mr. Hart) for about two years. Mr. Hart, a faithful member of the church that sponsored the college, had been very successful. For years he had pursued a rich man's hobby: collecting prize-winning big-game trophies he personally shot on hunting trips worldwide. His collection contained over 75 trophies, including a Bengal tiger, Cape buffalo, and kongoni antelope.

Mr. Redd, the college's fund-raising director, was, of course, aware of Mr. Hart's wealth. He was, however, only vaguely aware of his love of big-game hunting and of his trophy collection.

One day Dr. Jensen, curator of the college's life sciences collection, visited Mr. Redd and told him about Mr. Hart's big-game collection. (Dr. Jensen had only recently learned of the collection from a colleague.) Dr. Jensen suggested that perhaps Mr. Hart would consider giving the collection to the college. His reasoning was that the collection required a great deal of space in the Hart home, that Mr. Hart and his wife were getting on in years, and that the college would give the collection excellent care and expose it to thousands of people.

Mr. Redd had some reservations about Dr. Jensen's idea. First, he wasn't sure the college really wanted a collection of big-game trophies. And second, he was concerned about where the college would house the collection. "We really don't have a place that would do justice to something like that...we'd probably have to build something somewhere," he told Dr. Jensen.

Mr. Redd was, however, grateful for Dr. Jensen's visit, because it suggested a specific direction for future cultivational activities. Mr. Redd asked Dr. Jensen to begin sending Mr. Hart cultivational materials, including a newsletter, a series of articles about African big game, and a research paper on Alaskan wildlife. He urged Dr. Jensen to try to meet Mr. Hart and to earn his friendship and trust.

For years, Dr. Jensen had dreamed of a comprehensive, self-contained life sciences museum for the campus. Such a museum would facilitate research and make his excellent collections — everything from birds' eggs to beetles — readily accessible to researchers, students, and the public. (As things were, his collections were scattered in three different buildings, inadequately stored and protected, and not readily available for educational and research purposes.) Dr. Jensen saw in the Hart situation an opportunity to get the big-game trophies *and* his life sciences museum. His plan: Sell Mr. Hart on the idea of giving the college the trophies *and* of building a museum to house them.

Dr. Jensen set about in earnest to cultivate Mr. Hart. He sent the previously described materials with a cover letter in which he introduced himself and asked if he could visit Mr. Hart and see the collection. He said he would call Mr. Hart in a few days. About a week later, Dr. Jensen called Mr. Hart and reiterated his desire to see the collection. Mr. Hart was agreeable, and a week later Dr. Jensen was in Mr. Hart's home as his guest for two days. Before he left to visit Mr. Hart, however, Dr. Jensen learned everything he could about the man, including politics, hobbies, and interests besides hunting — plus the locations of all of his restaurants.

Within about three months, Dr. Jensen and Mr. Hart had become good friends. Each respected the knowledge and accomplishments of the other. Dr. Jensen, who had a doctorate in zoology, gave Mr. Hart some stimulating scientific insights into big game. Mr. Hart, on the other hand, enjoyed the attention Dr. Jensen gave him and the opportunity to associate with a respected member of academia. (Mr. Hart had never attended college.)

About six weeks after Dr. Jensen's visit to the Hart home, the zoologist succeeded in having Mr. Hart visit the campus as his guest. He introduced him to the college president, to his colleagues, and to Mr. Redd. He devoted two full days to showing him his marvelous collections. During this time, Dr. Jensen took Mr. Hart into his confidence. He told him of his dream to build a life sciences museum where the college's collections could be adequately, impressively displayed. He talked about the great research and educational value of specimens. And he pointed out that the college was ideally suited for a life sciences museum (there was not a good one in the entire state, and the college had a strong life sciences faculty and curriculum).

At this point, Mr. Hart responded almost on cue. He told Dr. Jensen he was going to donate his big-game collection to the college. Dr. Jensen reacted warmly to the news. He made it clear, however, that he was concerned about whether he should accept the collection in view of the fact that the college did not have a place to properly display it. (Mr. Hart had apparently assumed that if he donated his collection, the college would build the museum.) Dr. Jensen thanked Mr. Hart and told him he would be in touch with him about the matter.

Dr. Jensen then went to Mr. Redd and informed him of Mr. Hart's offer. Dr. Jensen asked Mr. Redd if he thought the college would be interested in having a life sciences museum if Mr. Hart built it. The college, of course, would donate the land and pay operating expenses. Mr. Redd felt that the college would be interested. He and Dr. Jensen subsequently met with the president and received his approval to make a proposal to Mr. Hart using that approach. They also received approval to name the museum the Reed F. Hart Life Sciences Museum.

With the help of the college physical plant department and the communications specialist on Mr. Redd's staff, Dr. Jensen began to prepare a request to Mr. Hart. It contained a site plan, floor plan (including square footage), equipment list, architectural renderings of the proposed museum, benefits of the museum to the college and community, and estimated cost. The name "Reed F. Hart Life Sciences Museum" appeared prominently on the building in the renderings.

Dr. Jensen and Mr. Redd met with Mr. Redd's planned-giving specialist (a CPA) to get advice on how Mr. Hart could best make the gift from a tax standpoint. Since most of Mr. Hart's wealth was in the restaurant stock he held, Dr. Jensen planned to suggest that Mr. Hart make a gift of appreciated property in the form of the stock.

During the three months the proposal was in preparation, Dr. Jensen continued to cultivate Mr. Hart. He made it clear that the college was grateful for his offer to donate the collection. He told Mr. Hart that a proposal was in preparation that would make it possible for the college to accept the collection and properly house it.

When the proposal was ready, Dr. Jensen made an appointment with Mr. Hart, and he (Dr. Jensen), Mr. Redd, and the college president met with Mr. Hart in his office. Using charts, the proposal proper, and other materials they had prepared, they outlined their plans for the museum. They were careful, however, to explain that they were flexible, and that *they wanted and needed Mr. Hart's ideas and suggestions.* They ended by asking for $3.5 million to build the museum. Mr. Hart was warm to the idea, but said he wanted time to consult with his financial advisers and to study it carefully.

Following the presentation, Dr. Jensen and the president maintained friendly, low-key contact with Mr. Hart. Several months went by with no firm decision from him. About six months after the presentation, Mr. Redd offered what proved to be an important suggestion. He noted that the college was about to launch a capital campaign in connection with the 75th anniversary of its founding. He suggested that they tell Mr. Hart that the college wanted to announce his gift at the kickoff banquet for the capital campaign. Such an announcement would get the campaign off to an excellent start and would encourage others to contribute. Subsequently, Dr. Jensen and the president jointly expressed that desire in a letter to Mr. Hart. They told him if he was agreable, they would honor him and his wife at the banquet.

Outcome. Mr. Hart agreed to give the college a total of $3.5 million in stock over five years. And he did, by the way, have some ideas of his own about how the museum should be built!

CASE HISTORY C

Mr. Wright, the fund raiser for a church-operated boys' home in the southeastern United States, was given a prospect referral by a member of the church. The prospect's name was Mr. Timms. He was a wealthy, 58-year-old inventor living in Kansas.

Significantly, Mr. Timms had spent his childhood in several foster homes, and both he and his wife were active members of the church that operated the boys' home for which Mr. Wright was raising funds.

Although Mr. Wright recognized that the home's distance from Mr. Timms was a major disadvantage, he felt the other factors made Mr. Timms an excellent prospect. His first step was to call the pastor of Mr. Timms' church in Kansas. Mr. Wright's call netted him two major benefits: 1) important additional information about Mr. Timms, and 2) a pledge from the pastor to help cultivate Mr. Timms to contribute to the boys' home. (Fortunately, Mr. Timms' local church was not operating a boys' home or any other institution that might have competed for his contribution.)

Mr. Wright then wrote a letter to Mr. Timms introducing himself and the boys' home. The letter was brief but offered some credible specifics, including the number of boys the home had helped in its 56 years of existence, and some of its needs. Mr. Wright also began sending Mr. Timms case histories of boys who had "graduated" from the home and had become responsible, contributing members of society.

Mr. Wright's cultivation effort was cut short, however, by a call from the pastor. He told Mr. Wright that Mr. Timms had suffered some financial reverses, and suggested that he cut back on his cultivational activities. Mr. Wright complied, although he did keep Mr. Timms on his distribution list for a quarterly newsletter.

Several years passed. Mr. Wright had almost forgotten about Mr. Timms. Then, out of the blue, Mr. Wright received a call from the pastor. His message: Mr. Timms had made a financial recovery and was once again a promising prospect. The pastor suggested that Mr. Wright resume full-scale cultivational activities, and, as before, he promised to assist.

Mr. Wright wrote Mr. Timms a second letter reintroducing himself and the boys' home. Again, he told Mr. Timms of the home's solid, documented accomplishments in helping young men. This time, however, Mr. Wright was able to add that the home was in the midst of a capital campaign to raise $500,000 to build an expanded facility with a shop and library. Mr. Wright was careful not to ask Mr. Timms for a contribution. He simply informed him of the home's activities and aspirations, and said that he would send along additional information from time to time. Mr. Wright realized that asking for the gift at this point — especially by mail — would have probably resulted in a token, "buy off" gift. Obviously, he didn't want that to happen.

About this time something happened that made Mr. Wright feel that God did, indeed, want the boys to have a new home: The home's baseball team won its regional playoff and qualified to play for the national championship. Playing site: Kansas City, Kansas — 20 miles from Mr. Timms' residence.

Mr. Wright quickly realized that the baseball team's trip to Kansas City offered some tremendous cultivational opportunities. It would, of course, give him a chance to meet Mr. Timms personally, talk to him about the boys' home and the campaign, "read" his reactions, and then tailor an approach to him for later presentation. But in addition, it would enable Mr. Wright to bring to bear some important, supplemental strategy involving:

- Arranging for Mr. Timms and his wife to be the home's guests at one of the ball games, sit with the national head of the church, and meet the ball players.

- Taking Mr. Timms and his wife to dinner where they would meet the founder and president of the boys' home and 10 "graduates" — all successful, established citizens. Each would give a brief, hopefully inspirational talk about how he felt about the boys' home. (Because of his age — 95 — and poor health, the boys' home president would not be attending any of the ball games.)

- Meeting with close friends and business associates of Mr. Timms who could help fill in some financial details. (Mr. Wright wasn't sure, for example, what form Mr. Timms' contribution should take. With additional information, he could ask an attorney to develop the best tax-planned giving approach.)

Ideally, Mr. Wright needed more time to cultivate Mr. Timms via mail and phone calls. The playoffs, however, were only two weeks away. He called the pastor, explained the situation, and asked his advice. The pastor recommended that Mr. Wright call Mr. Timms and invite him and his wife to the functions. The pastor said that he would prepare Mr. Timms for the call and do what he could to encourage a positive response.

After giving the pastor time to do his part, Mr. Wright called Mr. Timms and extended the ball-game and dinner invitations. Mr. Wright, wisely, was not coy with Mr. Timms. He told him that representatives of the home wanted to meet with him at some later date — after the Kansas meetings — to acquaint him further with the boys' home and some of its specific needs. (He had in mind inviting Mr. Timms and his wife to the home as special guests, but did not mention this on the phone.) Mr. Timms accepted the invitations.

After extensive work, and with the help of a volunteer who lived in Kansas City and the pastor, Mr. Wright completed all the arrangements. Once in Kansas City, he made an all-out effort to give the Timmses the red-carpet treatment. He and the pastor picked them up at their home, took a sincere interest in them, and extended them every proper courtesy. During the dinner, Mr. Wright learned that Mrs. Timms was interested in genealogy, and that she was attempting to trace her father's forebears whom she believed had lived in Virginia. He made a mental note to send her a newly available computerized list of everyone with the Green surname (her maiden name) who had lived in Virginia when federal censuses had been taken. Before the dinner was over, Mr. Wright had invited the Timmses to be his guests at the boys' home a month later. They accepted.

Between the Kansas City events and the Timmses' visit to the boys' home, Mr. Wright wrote two letters to them. The first was a warm thank-you note for the opportunity to meet with them and to enjoy their company. The second was a letter reminding them of their pending visit and asking for a specific arrival time, including airline and flight number. This letter included a postscript reading: "Mrs. Timms — You should receive shortly under separate cover a computerized list of all Greens who lived in Virginia during the 1800's. I hope this helps you trace your father's ancestors.''

With the help of a professional, freelance writer, Mr. Wright put together a presentation package that incorporated all the elements he felt would have maximum appeal to Mr. Timms. During his Kansas City visit, for example, he had learned that Mr. Timms was work-ethic oriented — that he felt contemporary young people needed to be taught how to work. Consequently, his proposal made specific mention of the fact that every boy in the home had a rotating schedule of chores to do six days a week.

The package also included a suggested way for Mr. Timms to make the gift based on what Mr. Wright had been able to learn in Kansas City about his financial situation. The suggested approach, prepared with an attorney's help, reflected estate planning and tax considerations.

When the Timmses arrived in Mr. Wright's city, he essentially repeated his Kansas City red-carpet treatment. He met them at the airport, took them to the home where they received a tour and met each boy, took them to dinner and then to their hotel. He told them that the national church leader they had met in Kansas City would be with them for lunch the next day, and that he would pick them up at 11:30.

Mr. Wright made the presentation at the lunch, but the church leader added some words of endorsement and support. The presentation included the suggestion that the expanded facility be named the "Stanley & Alice Timms Center." The attorney who had helped Mr. Wright prepare the presentation was at the luncheon and answered several questions that Mr. Timms asked.

Outcome. Mr. Timms placed appreciated securities worth $400,000 in an annuity trust for himself, his wife, and the boys' home. He and his wife receive annuity payments that increase their spendable income. In addition, they receive a charitable income-tax deduction, and the trust will avoid estate taxation when Mr. Timms dies. Mrs. Timms will receive annuity payments for however long she survives her husband. When she dies, the trust will end and the remaining assets will go to the boys' home.

8 ERI

If you can discover why people give, you can improve your fund-raising effectiveness. It is for this reason that the psychology of giving is analyzed in detail in Chapter 2. In a sense, this chapter is a continuation of Chapter 2, except that *donors* do the talking. In *their* words, they tell why they gave.

The author interviewed 12 donors who had contributed varying amounts in several different ways to a range of charitable organizations. To encourage frank responses, the donors were told that their comments would be kept confidential and published anonymously. Nevertheless, some of the donors' responses are probably less than candid. Even so, it is helpful to hear what donors *say* are the reasons why they gave, because if the donors are comfortable and secure with these reasons, then their responses merit our attention on that basis alone.

In fund raising, as in politics, medicine, law, and many other disciplines, there are "code" words and phrases exquisitely engineered to: A) conceal rather than reveal, B) sound good and be socially/professionally acceptable, and C) discourage further probing. Here are some examples of "code" words and phrases typically used by donors (watch for variations of these in the 12 donor statements on the pages that follow).

"We gave because we believe in the college and its educational program." (*Comment:* This may be true, but it probably wasn't *the* motivating force. Recognition, acceptance, tax benefits, and the other factors described in Chapter 2 must also be taken into account.)

"I agreed to publicity only so that others would know of my gift and be encouraged to make similar gifts." (*Comment:* Doubtful. This donor, typical of many donors, suggested that a photograph of him and the institutional president accompany the news release. In addition, he supplied a two-page biography and asked to receive all newspaper clippings. If his sole purpose in authorizing publicity was to promote the receiving organization, why didn't he ask that the news release omit his name and simply refer to him as an "anonymous donor"? This approach would have accomplished his expressed purpose of stimulating others to give. Obviously, this donor likes recognition but doesn't want to admit it.)

"I gave because I thought it was the right and proper thing to do." (*Comment:* Acceptable as a *partial* explanation. Unless the gift is a very small one, there's more to the story, and it can be found in one or more of the eight factors described in Chapter 2.)

"This contribution is our way of saying thanks for all the Center has done for our child." (*Comment:* Again, acceptable only as a *partial* explanation. It's likely that one of the chief factors that motivated the gift was a desire on the part of the parents to ensure that the Center would *continue* to help their child. This is a variation of the self-preservation element described in Chapter 2.)

Donor 1 (aged 36, land-developer). Gave his alma mater (a large, private university) controlling interest in a section of valuable coal-bearing land in Colorado. He restricted the gift to the College of Business. Potential value: into the tens of millions.

"I had a long-standing desire to help the university and the College of Business in particular. I owe much of my success to the preparation and insights my business professors gave me...I wanted to do something to pay them back. I think that my gift will make their business program even stronger. I would like to see them achieve national prominence. Tax considerations certainly made it easier and more attractive for me to give, and *were* a factor. Also, I like recognition...have a deep-seated need for it. I was pleased when the university asked about publicity and — with my approval — took photographs, wrote a news story, and released them to the media."

Donor 2 (aged 41, general contractor). Executed a will arranging for a major portion of his estate to pass to his alma mater (a junior college on the West Coast). His estate was valued at $4 million when the will was executed.

"I felt the college's church sponsor would advance the spiritual ideals on which I had based my life, and which had made me successful. The college has a strict program of spiritual training and high standards for faculty and students — I want to perpetuate these qualities...feel they are sadly lacking in contemporary America. I do not want all of my wealth to pass to my children. I think unearned wealth can destroy initiative...want my kids to work for what they get. I agreed to publicity for one reason: in the hope that my example will encourage others to make similar gifts to the college."

Donor 3 (aged 50, sports store owner in the northwest). Gave a fully equipped motor boat and three canoes to a parochial high school for use in a water sports course. Approximate value: $8,500.

"I'm basically stingy about donating, except where the church is concerned. I believe in their programs — both secular and ecclesiastical. I know that when I contribute to the church, they will use my money well. I am convinced that the teachers at the high school are dedicated, competent, and work hard for our young people. Recognition — a big article in the newspaper — is not important to me. I think it's counter to the Christian spirit of giving. And I don't think giving is necessarily good for my business. One of my customers who heard about my contribution said something like this to me: 'Well, if you can afford to give so much away, you probably don't need *my* business.' Another reason I gave is because I would rather control where my money goes than simply turn it over to the Internal Revenue Service. Our taxes breed the one thing we don't need more of — bureaucracy. And as far as I'm concerned, bureaucracy means more big government, big waste, and wild-eyed social programs that take away people's incentive to work."

Donor 4 (aged 64, Florida gynecologist). Established a unitrust for herself and the hospital with which she was affiliated for much of her professional life. She transferred to the hospital in trust

$60,000 worth of securities. Each year the value of the trust assets is determined by the trustees, and the donor receives a fixed percentage of that value.

"I had a threefold motivation — I wanted some tax relief, wanted to contibute to the hospital, and wanted to assure myself of continuing spendable income. Tax relief took the form of a charitable contribution deduction on my income tax, avoidance of capital gains tax, and some estate tax benefits when I die. The hospital will receive the value of the trust assets when I'm gone. I have long felt obligated to the hospital: It was the source of my livelihood and the place where I built my professional reputation. I want to be well thought of by my associates, patients, and others...want to be remembered in a positive way. I believe the hospital is a good one. I want to see it maintain its excellence, and perhaps do more in research. Also, I felt some pressure to give: Many of my associates have given comparable gifts."

Donor 5 (aged 27, Chicago sheet metal worker). Pledged $20 to a policeman's benefit association in response to a telephone solicitation.

"It's hard for me to say no when someone wants my help...when they come right out and ask me. I want people to like me. I feel that I have failed or fallen short in some way when I refuse to help people. I'd rather pay the $20 than feel bad about it for several days because I didn't pay it. Twenty dollars isn't very much...I can handle that much. I think the police here work hard and deserve a little help. They have a tough job, really, and they earn every bit of what they get. Besides, the person who called was a woman with a *great* voice. I couldn't say no to that!"

Donor 6 (aged 46, owner of a fast-food restaurant). Gave a nearby college $500 cash (unrestricted) and pledged an additional $500 each year for five years. He was awarded membership in the college's President's Club for his contribution and received a plaque. He displays the plaque in a prominent place in his restaurant.

"I give for different reasons at different times. In this case, I gave mainly because I feel that I owe the college something. Most of my customers are students at the college, and they have been good to me...made me successful. I wanted to return the favor — do something to help their institution. So it was, I guess, a 'business decision.' I might add, though, that I believe in the college. I think it is a good influence in the community. I'm comfortable giving them my money. I would say that tax considerations are a subordinate factor in my giving. Tax breaks encourage me to give — reinforce my tendency to give, but they are not the primary factor.''

Donor 7 (aged 61, college botany professor). Gave his New England college an outright gift of an apartment house valued at $300,000. He stipulated that the college sell the apartment house and use the proceeds to establish a scholarship fund for nursing students. The fund carries the name of his mother. Interest earned on the principal provides full tuition and fees for eight nursing students each year.

''My mother was a nurse — a noble, wonderful, dedicated nurse. She worked very hard, and also served as a midwife. I wanted to honor her memory and to give financial help to young women interested in nursing careers. I was comfortable giving to the nursing program for another reason: The dean there enjoys a lot of autonomy — isn't all wrapped up in administrative politics, paperwork, and red tape. I knew that my money would be used efficiently and for the use I intended. Tax factors didn't make me decide to give — they just made it easier for me to do so. I asked for some publicity...felt I deserved it. Also, I hoped the publicity would stimulate gifts for the college from others.''

Donor 8 (aged 52, owner of a medium-sized grocery store). Gave $2,500 in cash to a boys' club to help them build a new club house.

''My brother says I've always given everything away...been too free with my belongings. He says I've always gone overboard. I don't know. I guess I feel bad for those kids whose parents have sort of copped out on them. When the boys' club president and two of the boys visited me and asked for the money, I just didn't want to refuse. I felt good that they would think of me in that way — as somebody who would be willing to help...do a good thing like that. They made me feel important, and I just couldn't let them down. Giving to them really gave me a lift — joy, I guess, is the word. You know, after you make some big purchase — new car, boat, something like that — you feel blue about it for days afterward, wondering if you did the right thing. But after I gave that $2,500, it wasn't that way. It was just a great feeling, and the feeling comes back every time I think about it.''

Donor 9 (aged 48, Pennsylvania home-builder). Gave $25,000 cash over a three-year period to help finance an addition to a local hospital.

"That hospital is part of me and my family...reaches back to my grandparents. I was born there, my grandfather and father died there. My kids were born there. The hospital has always been there when we needed it. It seemed funny for the *hospital,* all of a sudden, to need *me.* The people who asked me to give — the director and one of the doctors — were right out with it. They said they needed $25,000 from successful members of the community and would I give. In a tactful way they pointed out what the hospital had given me and would continue to give me and my family in the future. They said the expansion would result in better facilities, better health care. I was wavering a bit. Then they talked about some tax advantages, and showed me how my gift would affect my taxes (they had really scouted me!). After I consulted with my own attorney, which they encouraged me to do, I decided to give. Boiled down, it was a matter of discharging an obligation I felt to the hospital in a way that wasn't too painful. Part of it, too, was the fact that I was helping people in the community who had given me my livelihood by buying houses from me.''

Donor 10 (aged 67, housewife and widow). Gave $11,200 cash to improve agriculture on an American Indian reservation in Arizona.

"My late husband and I worked with the Indian people throughout the Southwest for many years. He was with a governmental Indian agency, and I took an active interest in his work. We both came to respect and love the Indian people. He and I never talked about it openly, but I think we both felt guilty about our family having so much more than the Indians — materially, I mean. I decided that I wanted to do *something* to help them. Agriculture seemed like a sensible philanthropic investment...something that would literally reap dividends. The disability and mortality rates of American Indians are still shamefully high. With good agriculture, however, they can improve their health and perhaps develop another source of income to improve their standard of living.''

Donor 11 (aged 44, prominent California dentist). Gave $15,000 cash to a university special-gift club devoted to athletics. His contribution entitled him to lifetime membership in the club and to several worthwhile benefits, including VIP treatment for parking and tickets.

''I was going to lose the money anyway — if not to the athletic club, then to Uncle Sam. By giving to the club, I had some say about where my money went, and I got some privileges that I enjoy and — frankly — that are good for my professional image. This is probably going to sound bad, but you asked me to be honest: You see, it's important for professional people to have the accouterments of success...yes, even to be seen sitting in good seats at a basketball game! I recognize that. It's a lot like life insurance salesmen driving Cadillacs...good for business. I don't think, though, that my contribution was without charitable intent. I was pleased to be able to help promote the university through athletics. After all, I did my undergraduate work at that school. They are the people who got me started.''

Donor 12 (aged 63, New York television executive). Placed his $600,000 estate in a marital deduction trust and a unitrust, taking advantage of both marital and charitable deductions. This arrangement will eliminate federal estate tax on the executive's estate when he dies, and may well eliminate estate tax on his wife's estate upon her death. When she dies, the principal of one of the trusts will go as her will directs; the principal of the other trust will go to their church.

''We didn't set out to give money to our church. Rather, my wife and I went to our attorney for some estate-planning help. It was he who made us aware of the fact that we could conserve our estate and help our church at the same time. I was aware of the fact that the church was looking to me for some financial help, but my first concern was to take care of my wife and our children. When it became clear that helping the church was in some ways supportive of what I wanted to do for my wife and family — well, that clinched it. I've thought about other aspects of why I gave, and I've really tried to analyze it honestly. Maybe this isn't profound, but it seems to me that when people get into their 60's or so, they feel the world is leaving them behind — which, of course, it is. They feel their influence and power ebbing, especially if they've had some influence and power in their younger years. So it seems to me that giving in one's sunset years is one way to have some impact — wield some power, if you will — when physically, mentally, and position-wise you're beginning to *lose* power. Maybe giving is a way to strike back in your declining years...maybe a way to soften the swing of the grim reaper."

9 ▦ FRI

ADVICE FROM VETERANS

...men are my teachers.
—PLATO

Fund raisers would do well to adapt Plato's statement to read, "Other fund raisers are my teachers." The point is, of course, that fund raising takes in so much territory and encompasses so many skills that no one person's experience can ever be enough.

With that in mind, the author turned to respected, established fund raisers across the country for their ideas about the art of asking. Specifically, they were asked to respond to this question: "If you had only a few minutes to counsel someone about fund raising — a person with little to moderate fund-raising experience — what would you tell him or her?"

Their responses, which follow, were warmly and graciously given, and reflected a sincere desire to be helpful. What they say covers a remarkable range of concerns and provides convincing evidence that fund raising is, indeed, an eclectic, diverse discipline.

Helen L. O'Rourke (Vice President, Philanthropic Advisory Service, Council of Better Business Bureaus). "Americans are generous people — they want to give to charities. And they will continue to contribute as long as fund raisers don't abuse their faith. A fund raiser has to build trust — donors must feel confident that when a fund raiser promises that their dollars will help needy children or build a theater, these things will happen. Nothing alienates donors more quickly than the feeling they've been duped or misled by a fund raiser. And then some donors are just naturally wary of fund raisers, suspecting them of making too large a profit.

"To counter this mistrust and to build faith, a fund raiser must be credible and accountable. This means full disclosure and informing donors of the results of your campaigns. Let them know what happened to their donations. Be open about your finances. Account for their dollars, even those that pay for fund raising and administration. In short, accountability creates credibility which means greater fund-raising success."

Neal H. Hurwitz (fund-raising management consultant). "The first step in fund raising is to determine your need. In so doing, you must be very clear about your program and purposes. Lack of clarity, confusion, trying to accomplish too much or too little — these are all dangers to avoid.

"In thinking rationally about needs, you may start from an emotional base. (For example: 'These people are starving and that makes me feel so bad so I want to help them and get others to do so, too'; or 'This facility is crucial for our treatment program and without it we will not be able to meet the needs of many people — let's get it built and soon!') Starting from a sense of urgent need yourself, you must then think rationally about how to communicate that need to others so that they will share your feelings and sense of urgency, and contribute to your proposed solution (new building, feeding program, etc.).

"Having carefully identified your needs, you proceed to consider *all* possible sources of funding: individuals, community groups and organizations, foundations, government agencies, corporations and small businesses, etc. Brainstorm, make lists, think boldly and creatively, don't prejudge, assume that everyone is (at least potentially) on your side, for your cause, concerned about your needs and objectives.

"Next, you need to test your prospective funding sources. This is where efficiency and careful monitoring of use of resources are crucial. If you can afford it, seek professional advice from a fund-raising consultant. If you cannot afford professional help, start small and work your way up. Write letters to foundations and tell them what you want to do. Ask for their reports and guidelines so that you know what *they* are looking for in worthwhile projects. Contact members of your board of trustees or advisory council; ask them for leads among corporations, foundations, and small businesses. Send appeal letters to selected lists of people who may be sympathetic to your cause. Ask past contributors to increase their gifts in the present.

"Obviously, professional advice can save you money if you are ineffective in your fund-raising efforts. On the other hand, skilled administrators and laypersons with good ideas have often been quite successful on their own. Each situation is unique to some extent; each must be appraised on its own merits.

"Finally, once the fund-raising program is established and going, all of the above elements are endlessly repeated. Continue to determine needs and make them attractive to potential givers. Design fund-raising programs that bring in the most dollars for the least cost. These are the basics of successful fund raising."

Conrad Squires (President, The National Copy Clinic, Inc.)
"When you are writing to ask someone for money, write simply, modestly, honestly. Be specific about what you want. Be cheerful. Write a warm letter — let your humaneness show. Care. Give your reader an opportunity to care, too.

"Everyone wants to think well of himself or herself — offer the reader an opportunity to strengthen his or her self-image as someone willing to help others. Ask for specific amounts. Suggest a range of gifts if you are writing to people of different economic levels. Do not say more than you have to say to complete your argument. Do not say less, either — assume the reader knows little about your institution.

"Write to an individual, not to a crowd. Take your time when you are writing. If you don't like to write, find someone who does. Revise your letter until it is as good as you can make it. Then show your letter to people whose intelligence you respect. Listen to them. Rest the material for a day or two. Then revise it to eliminate any major flaws you find, and to make it more persuasive, simpler, and quicker to read.

"Be sure you mail a return vehicle that will identify the donor properly — a card or reply envelope that is either pre-addressed or has spaces for name, address, etc. And do not stop with a single mailing. Send at least one follow-up. If you do not, you will assuredly miss some income that would have reached you. Finally, be sure to thank the donor."

Brian O'Connell (President, Independent Sector, writing in "Effective Leadership in Voluntary Organizations"). "Fund-raising campaigns can be fun. They are almost always exciting. They provide a rallying point for the organization and in many ways lend an air of excitement to the whole operation.

"They're also hard work! And sustaining the effort year in and year out is particularly tough. You'll need to carefully and quickly promote volunteers up through the campaign organization (and surely from the campaign organization to the board) so that there can be new blood and fresh leadership moving forward to share in the excitement of the campaign and thus be stimulated to carry the burdens of it for a while.

"Fund raising has to be high on the board's agenda and high in status and recognition within the agency. A successful fund-raising performance has to be acknowledged and applauded throughout the organization. Find every possible way to say 'thank you' and to give people the warm feeling of accomplishment to which they are entitled and which all human beings desire. When I was with the American Heart Association in Baltimore, every year we sent a New Year's card to every one of the 7,000 block workers with a message something like this: 'During the season of good will we want to thank you again for your wonderful service to your community as a Heart Association volunteer.'

"People want a cause. You have to help your people to realize that they've got an awfully good one that is not only doing great things, but that is also grateful for the campaign volunteer's efforts."

Byron Welch (President, Welch Associates, Inc.) "Essential to success in fund-raising management are elements common to success in living. These elements include integrity, character, enthusiasm, judgment, knowledge, resourcefulness, and persistence. Perhaps persistent integrity would be the perfect mix of them all. Nothing in all of the world can take the place of trying again and again. This presupposes integrity — institutional honesty, factual need, and case; individual integrity — doing what you can, and honestly following through on every promise of service and support.

"Without integrity it is pointless to keep on trying. Constant self-examination of program will keep the institution honest, if self-study is done to improve the quality of the service to the served publics. Constant self-improvement of one's skills in communication, logic, motivation, and purpose — if done to be a better professional tomorrow than one is today — will do more ultimately to serve an institution, and the giving public as well, than a thousand finely turned phrases in a case statement.

"Remembering Albert Pine's admonition that what we do for ourselves dies with us, and that only what we do for others will remain and become immortal, I would want every fund-raising manager to be selfless in his or her service. I would like all of us in this profession to feel that we belong to something bigger than ourselves; that we can and do work with others to achieve worthy goals which alone could not be achieved; that we each do our own part, cheerfully; that we know the pride felt in a job well done, and take our moment of glory in humility when (and if) it ever comes; that we are willing to work hard to make our ideas take shape, and that we are in fact helping to build things of lasting value.

"When Huey Long lay dying from an assassin's bullet in September 1935, his final words were, 'God, don't let me die. I have so much to do.' So do I; so do you. Given the opportunities of the fund-raising manager today and into the future, we ought to be able to say we have done our best to make our world a more fit place for another to enjoy."

Robert M. Holcombe (Assistant Vice President/Development, Lehigh University). "Your first responsibility in fund raising is to understand the needs of your institution and explain them in a convincing manner to your constituency. To explain these needs, you should develop what is called the 'case statement.' This statement must be clear and persuasive in outlining the needs and objectives of your program. Donors are becoming more sophisticated and want to be assured that an institution's needs are urgent and well conceived.

"Your next important step in a major solicitation is to bring the right persons together; that is, to have the right solicitor contact the prospective donor. This was brought home to me in a solicitation for our capital campaign in which we thought for two months about who should call on a certain prospect. After making a suggestion, our president and one of our key trustees made the call. The prospect made the requested commitment immediately and indicated that he knew the president had to be there, but that he was particularly pleased that the trustee had flown 500 miles to make the call. As this case illustrates, the need was made clear, the right persons made the call, and the donor responded."

Stephen Wertheimer (Vice President for Development, Baruch College). "The best advice to a new fund raiser preparing a campaign plan is: Think like the prospects.

"Prospects have tough questions on their minds. Most of them won't take the trouble to ask these questions; it's your responsibility to anticipate them and provide the answers. Prospects want assurance that the people and organization sponsoring the appeal can accomplish the objective for which they are raising money. They want facts that create a credible basis for support of the cause or appeal. Hopes, wishes, and ideals must be linked to rational, achievable, and necessary objectives.

"Prospects want to be perceived as *people,* not as cards, lists, or a mass. People *do* give to people — provided they make the right request. Prospects want to hear 'you' more than 'need'. There should be pride in giving, so prospects lean to dignified appeals and eschew mere beggary, sensationalism, or emotionalism.

"Most prospects want to join their gift with others to make giving effective; they need assurance their gift is sought in a spirit of universalism among all who should be asked. No one wants to end up as a lone donor.

"If you are satisfied with the answers you give to yourself, the campaign is probably off to a good start."

Charles E. Lawson (President, Treasurer, and Managing Partner; Brakeley, John Price Jones Inc.) "My advice to the newcomer to the fund-raising profession is to volunteer to work in a fund-raising campaign for an organization other than the one that employs him or her. There really is no substitute for the actual experience of 'giving' and 'asking' in behalf of a worthy cause. Once professionals have gained that experience, they can comfortably place themselves in the shoes of the volunteer solicitor — a perspective that will prove to be a great advantage in counseling or managing volunteer fund raisers. They will then readily grasp the importance of Lawson's Thirteen Tips for Successful Solicitation, to wit:

- "Remember that the best of all worlds is a solicitation conducted by the right person, at the right time, in the right place, for the right cause, at the right amount, and in the right manner.

- "Be familiar with the reasons why people give.

- "Keep in mind that the successful solicitor will know his or her prospect through adequate research about his or her interests, linkages, and capacity to give.

- "Bear in mind that both giving and receiving are privileges and not rights. The donor's obligation to be a good steward of his or her philanthropy is as important as the recipient organization's stewardship of funds received.

- "View the 'first ask' as a step in the cultivation process. Don't be discouraged if you receive a negative response the first time around, but do take a third 'no' seriously.

- "Be aware that gifts are only one category in the prospective donor's catalog of discretionary expenditures and that the competition for those discretionary dollars is, therefore, keen. The successful solicitor is involved in the process of shifting the prospect's priorities and, therefore, must be prepared to provide him or her with sufficient reasons for reshuffling priorities — including the rewards the donor will enjoy as a result of giving.

- "Acknowledge that giving is a very personal experience and every approach from the point of the first contact through the 'thank you' and reports on stewardship of the donor's investment should be treated accordingly.

- "Encourage the solicitor to be prepared to suggest a level of giving either directly, through his or her own example, the example of others, or a combination of all three — the solicitor will be doing the prospective donor a favor.

- "Ensure that the solicitor understands that the prospective donor will believe that the gift will be only as important as the asker treats it.

- "In effective pairing of solicitors to prospects, be sure the asker has given himself at a level equal to or in excess (in proportion to his means) of that to be asked of the prospective donor.

- "Prepare the asker to state the specific reasons he gave as well as the reasons he believes the prospect should give.

- "Be sure that every asker has pride in his or her task and remember that a solicitation should be an enjoyable experience for all involved.

- "Whenever possible, outnumber the prospect with members of the solicitation team — the response to a request is quite often reflective of the ratio of askers to the potential donor."

Ralph E. Chamberlain (Director of Development, The Salvation Army, Greater New York Division). "If I had to give one piece of advice to a truly neophyte fund raiser it would have to be: 'Use your common sense.'

"So much of our professional activity is based on down-to-earth common sense. Common sense tells you that people will not give unless they are asked. Common sense tells you that there has to be a reason for the gift. Common sense tells you that after the gift is received, the donor should be thanked.

"We, who have been in the profession for more years than we would care to mention, sometimes allow ourselves to get a bit carried away with the more esoteric aspects of our field. But, when the rhetoric sifts away, so much of what we do is simply a logical progression.

"To the neophyte, I would say read as much as you can; attend what educational seminars you can; learn from whomever is available to you *but* when all else fails...use your common sense."

Ellen G. Estes (attorney and planned giving consultant). "Although it is difficult to give meaningful advice in only a few words, my emphasis would be as follows: Learn about your organization and think about how to convey its story in a positive and compelling way to your constituency. You should, of course, learn the basic techniques of fund raising, but the most important part — the part that is most challenging and fun — is the interaction with people. Fund raising is, after all, a 'people' business, whether it be talking with corporate or foundation representatives, or working with individual prospects.

"You should make it your business to let your prospects know that you care about *their* needs, goals, and concerns, as well as those of your organization. Involving prospects with your organization in a way that reflects their interests can produce positive results — in terms of good will, enthusiasm, and meaningful gifts. Keep in mind that a little sensitivity and flexibility, as well as creativity in working out gift arrangements for your mutual benefit, will go a long, long way."

William C. McGinly (Executive Director, National Association for Hospital Development). "The reasons why people donate and volunteer are as varied as the people themselves, and I'd suggest that many newcomers to fund raising (and some of the pros as well) miss one of the most compelling reasons.

"While even the toughest prospects are often approached with an appeal based upon what's required to meet the fund raiser's needs and the institution's program expectations, consummate fund raisers don't just have facts available to make the appeal for their cause. The real pros achieve success by listening well. By putting themselves in the prospect's shoes, these fund raisers successfully match the prospects' needs with the institutions'.

"By searching out the unique needs and interests of prospects and by appealing to them in meaningful ways, the fund raiser can create an exchange in which the tangible gift is bartered for that intangible satisfaction of contributing and giving. Not satisfying the donor's need is one reason the best of causes often go wanting. Once the neophyte recognizes the importance of discovering and responding to the needs of the donor, he or she is providing meaningful satisfaction to all parties.

"If I were to sum it up for the beginner, I'd simply suggest working to establish an exchange between the donor and the institution by identifying and meeting the donor's need. Placing the donor's requirements first will ensure success in a continued and long-lasting fashion."

J. Richard Wilson (President, National Society of Fund-Raising Executives). "Here are some basic suggestions for someone new to fund raising.

- "Devote a great deal of time and patience to the planning process. If you are not satisfied with your plan, then you should delay the start of the fund-raising effort. A good plan is essential to fund-raising success. If you don't know where you're going, you never are going to get there!

- "Remember that you can't do the job alone. Involve volunteers in a very real way. Make them part of the planning process to the extent that they feel it is *their* plan, too. And keep them close to you throughout the fund-raising effort, sharing your success and disappointments.

- "An important part of successful fund raising is to develop the base of prospects. This requires some imagination. Think of all the reasons why someone should give to your cause. This will open up new ideas for sources of prospects. Again, your volunteers can help significantly in this process.

- "Don't take on anything more than what you can do well. The quality of your fund-raising effort is a reflection of the quality of your organization. People exposed to your fund-raising effort for the first time will quickly decide whether they want to stay involved.

- "Total integrity in everything you do in the fund-raising process is absolutely essential. Not only your credibility as a person, but the credibility of your cause is at stake.

- "After (and during) any fund-raising effort, it is important to evaluate and note your successes and failures. Try to determine why things happened as they did, and this will lead to a better plan for the next time.

- "Always be positive. People want to be part of something that is moving forward...something successful. People do not stay involved with something where there are doubts, questions, and false starts.

- "Seek the advice of an experienced fund-raising executive and share with him or her your plans. (It is easy to meet someone willing to help at an NSFRE meeting.) Don't be afraid to ask, and to share your problems. You will be surprised at how willing people are to help you."

Donald T. Nelson (former Director, LDS Foundation). "Volunteers have contributed importantly to the success of American philanthropy. No one can really argue with that. They have walked, washed, called, baked, danced, pleaded, raced, and performed in countless other ways in from-the-heart efforts to raise funds for everything from Little League uniforms to music halls and higher education.

"Nevertheless, you should recognize that unless you choose your volunteers carefully and keep them to the minimum number needed, you may well end up serving them rather than having them serve your cause. Some volunteers will consume a great deal of your time, energy, and patience. Some will expect certain material dividends. Some will have their feelings hurt and turn on you and your cause.

"Moral: Be selective about choosing and using volunteers. Look for stability, maturity, and a good sense of responsibility. Recruit from your own circle of friends, and then recruit their friends. Have volunteers do only those things that the professional staff cannot do. Make volunteers' work quick, easy, and rewarding, and they will stay with you. If you take these precautions, you will be on your way to establishing a strong, productive fund-raising organization from the ground up."

Howard M. Schwartz (former fund-raising consultant). "I am constantly amazed at the number of significant institutions and organizations that plan and implement fund-raising programs without consideration for, or even understanding of, what I consider to be the entire essence of the profession — marketing!

"Fund raising is but the nonprofit world's equivalent of selling, except instead of a physical product to be offered in the marketplace, the offering is of an idea or concept. American business has very sharply refined the process of marketing, with little doubt left as to probable results after proper consumer research is undertaken, good sales strategy established, effective advertising and promotion initiated, and the sales force trained and provided with necessary aids.

"Most nonprofit groups would benefit by emulating the marketing practices of business and industry. It is totally erroneous to assume that because a charity is a good one and meets a community need it will be supported. In 20 years of fund raising I saw this 'I deserve support and therefore will get it' attitude over and over again. But successful programs must be built on a solid base of understanding the prospect (research), developing the right cultivation process (advertising), and effectively evoking support (sales)."

10 ERI   PROFESSIONAL STANDARDS AND GOVERNMENT REGULATIONS

Philanthropic fund raising, like public office, is a public trust. Fund raisers depend upon the public for their support, and — if their charities are properly managed — they use that support in the public interest. In a very real sense, then, such fund raisers are brokers for the public welfare. Consequently, it is right and reasonable that they be accountable to their publics and to the governments under whose aegis they operate.

This chapter introduces you to professional standards and government regulations affecting fund raising in the United States. The intent is not merely to make you aware of the spirit, and — in some cases — the letter of the law, but also to make you a better fund raiser. Compliance with standards and with intelligently legislated regulation will, inevitably, enhance public confidence and participation in the philanthropic process.

We'll look at standards first. Over the years, several organizations have promoted constructive standards of fund-raising conduct. Two stand out: the National Charities Information Bureau, Inc., and the Council of Better Business Bureaus, Inc. Their recommended standards are practical, positive, and sensitive to the needs of both givers and receivers, and — in many cases — consistent with existing and pending governmental regulation. So you should learn them and make them a part of your way of doing philanthropic business.

NATIONAL CHARITIES INFORMATION BUREAU, INC.

The NCIB, formerly known as the National Information Bureau, was established in 1918. It is a "not-for-profit, independent watchdog organization" formed "to help keep philanthropies in its field true to the ideals and standards that should characterize all charitable organizations." The NCIB has publicly challenged the practices of certain charities — even the giants — and has exposed alleged abuses. The organization issues a monthly bulletin, Wise Giving Guide, in which it evaluates hundreds of national charities against eight NCIB standards. Fair-minded fund raisers will find these standards, which are, of course, subject to revision, to be functional and deserving of their support. These are the NCIB Basic Standards in Philanthropy, reproduced here with the permission of the NCIB.

Philanthropic organizations have a high degree of responsibility because of the public trusteeship involved. Compliance with the following standards, with reasonable evidence supplied on request, is considered essential for approval by the NCIB.

Board. An active and responsible governing body, holding regular meetings, whose members have no material conflict of interest and serve without compensation.

Purpose. A clear statement of purpose in the public interest.

Program. A program consistent with the organization's stated purpose and its personnel and financial resources, and involving interagency cooperation to avoid duplication of work.

Expenses. Reasonable program, management, and fund-raising expenses.

Promotion. Ethical publicity and promotion excluding exaggerated or misleading claims.

Fund raising. Solicitation of contributions without payment of commissions or undue pressure (such as mailing unordered tickets or merchandise, general telephone solicitation, and use of identified government employees as solicitors).

Accountability. An annual report available on request that describes program activities and supporting services in relation to expenses and that contains financial statements comprising a balance sheet, a statement of support/revenue and expenses and changes in fund balances, a statement of functional expenses, and notes to financial statements, that are accompanied by the report of an independent public accountant. National organizations operating with affiliates should provide combined or acceptably compiled financial statements prepared in the foregoing manner. For its analysis NCIB may request disclosure of accounting treatment of various items included in the financial statements.

Budget. Detailed annual budget approved by the governing body in a form consistent with annual financial statements.

COUNCIL OF BETTER BUSINESS BUREAUS, INC.

In 1974 the Council of Better Business Bureaus, Inc., published an important, perhaps even a landmark document: Standards for Charitable Solicitations. These standards were prepared under the direction of the Philanthropic Advisory Service, a division of the CBBB established to promote ethical standards and public accountability among nonprofit organizations. The document embodied the thinking of hundreds of communicators, charity officers, professional fund raisers, accountants, direct-mail specialists, government officials, and advisers from a cross section of American life.

Unquestionably, the standards this document set forth were the most comprehensive and detailed ever offered to American charities and their publics. They were developed to facilitate, not to frustrate, legitimate fund-raising activities. Their purpose was to encourage candor, integrity, and accountability among charities and more informed giving decisions among donors — a purpose that continues today.

In 1977, the CBBB published expanded and strengthened standards under the same title as those issued originally. These standards — as did the original ones — pointed the way to more meaningful, rewarding, and fulfilling fund raising for those who ask and for those who give. In 1982, the CBBB condensed and consolidated the 55 original standards into a more manageable 22. If you tend to think principally in practical terms, be reassured: Compliance with these CBBB standards is virtually certain to contribute to your fund-raising success.

Like the NCIB, the CBBB also publishes a report, Give But Give Wisely, issued quarterly, in which it lists charities generating the most inquiries to the CBBB. The report indicates whether specific charities do or do not comply with CBBB standards. In addition, the CBBB prepares detailed summaries on individual soliciting organizations whose programs or fund-raising efforts are national or international in scope. Each report includes information about the charity's background, activities, governance, fund raising and finances, as well as an explanation of whether the group's practices meet CBBB standards.

The following are the Standards for Charitable Solicitations published in 1982 by the Council of Better Business Bureaus, Inc. This text is copyrighted by the Council and is reproduced here with the Council's permission.

Introduction. The Council of Better Business Bureaus promulgates these standards to promote ethical practices by philanthropic organizations. The Council of Better Business Bureaus believes that adherence to these standards by soliciting organizations will inspire public confidence, further the growth of public participation in philanthropy, and advance the objectives of responsible private initiative and self-regulation. Both the public and soliciting organizations will benefit from voluntary disclosure of an organization's activities, finances, fund-raising practices, and governance — information that donors and prospective donors will reasonably wish to consider. These standards apply to publicly soliciting organizations that are tax exempt under section 501(c)(3) of the Internal Revenue Code, and to other organizations conducting charitable solicitations.

While the Council of Better Business Bureaus and its member Better Business Bureaus generally do not report on schools, colleges, or churches soliciting within their congregations, they encourage all soliciting organizations to adhere to these standards. These standards were developed with professional and technical assistance from representatives of soliciting organizations, professional fund-raising firms and associations, the accounting profession, corporate contributions officers, regulatory agencies, and the Better Business Bureau system. The Council of Better Business Bureaus is solely responsible for the contents of these standards.

For the purposes of these standards:

1) "Charitable solicitation" (or "solicitation") is any direct or indirect request for money, property, credit, volunteer service or other thing of value, to be given now or on a deferred basis, on the representation that it will be used for charitable, educational, religious, benevolent, patriotic, civic, or other philanthropic purposes. Solicitations include invitations to voting membership and appeals to voting members when a contribution is a principal requirement for membership.

2) "Soliciting organization" (or "organization") is any corporation, trust, group, partnership, or individual engaged in a charitable solicitation; a "solicitor" is anyone engaged in a charitable solicitation.

3) The "public" includes individuals, groups, associations, corporations, foundations, institutions, and/or government agencies.

4) "Fund raising" includes a charitable solicitation, the activities, representations, and materials which are an integral part of the planning, creation, production, and communication of the solicitation; and the collection of the money, property, or other thing of value requested. Fund raising includes but is not limited to donor acquisition and renewal, development, fund or resource development, member or membership development, and contract or grant procurement.

Public accountability • Soliciting organizations shall provide on request an annual report. The annual report, an annually-updated written account, shall present the organization's purposes; descriptions of overall programs, activities and accomplishments; eligibility to receive deductible contributions; information about the governing body and structure; and information about financial activities and financial position.

• Soliciting organizations shall provide on request complete annual financial statements. The financial statements shall present the overall financial activities and financial position of the organization, shall be prepared in accordance with generally accepted accounting principles and reporting practices, and shall include the auditor's or treasurer's report, notes, and any supplementary schedules. When total annual income exceeds $100,000, the financial statements shall be audited in accordance with generally accepted auditing standards.

• Soliciting organizations' financial statements shall present adequate information to serve as a basis for informed decisions. Information needed as a basis for informed decisions generally includes but is not limited to: a) significant categories of contributions and other income; b) expenses reported in categories corresponding to the descriptions of major programs and activities contained in the annual report, solicitations, and other informational materials; c) a detailed schedule of expenses by natural classification (e.g., salaries, employee benefits, occupancy, postage, etc.), presenting the natural expenses incurred for each major program and supporting activity; d) accurate presentation of all fund-raising and administrative costs; and e) when a significant activity combines fund raising and one or more other purposes (e.g., door-to-door canvassing combining fund raising and social advocacy, or television broadcasts combining fund raising and religious ministry, or a direct mail campaign combining fund raising and public education), the financial statements shall specify the total cost of the multi-purpose activity and the basis for allocating its costs.

• Organizations receiving a substantial portion of their income through the fund-raising activities of controlled or affiliated entities shall provide on request an accounting of all income received by and fund-raising costs incurred by such entities. Such entities include committees, branches or chapters which are controlled by or affiliated with the benefiting organization, and for which a primary activity is raising funds to support the programs of the benefiting organization.

Use of funds • A reasonable percentage of total income from all sources shall be applied to programs and activities directly related to the purposes for which the organization exists • A reasonable percentage of public contributions shall be applied to the programs and activities described in solicitations, in accordance with donor expectations • Fund-raising costs shall be reasonable.

• Total fund-raising and administrative costs shall be reasonable. Reasonable use of funds requires that: a) at least 50 percent of total income from all sources be spent on programs and activities directly related to the organization's purposes; b) at least 50 percent of public contributions be spent on the programs and activities described in solicitations, in accordance with donor expectations; c) fund-raising costs not exceed 35 percent of related contributions; and d) total fund-raising and administrative costs not exceed 50 percent of total income. An organization which does not meet one or more of these percentage limitations may provide evidence to demonstrate that its use of funds is reasonable. The higher fund-raising and administrative costs of a newly created organization, donor restrictions on the use of funds, exceptional bequests, a stigma associated with a cause, and environmental or political events beyond an organization's control are among the factors which may result in costs that are reasonable although they do not meet these percentage limitations • Soliciting organizations shall substantiate on request their application of funds, in accordance with donor expectations, to the programs and activities described in solicitations • Soliciting organizations shall establish and exercise adequate controls over disbursements.

Solicitations and informational materials • Solicitations and informational materials, distributed by any means, shall be accurate, truthful and not misleading, both in whole and in part. • Soliciting organizations shall substantiate on request that solicitations and informational materials, distributed by any means, are accurate, truthful and not misleading, in whole and in part • Solicitations shall include a clear description of the programs and activities for which funds are requested. Solicitations which describe an issue, problem, need or event, but which do not clearly describe the programs or activities for which funds are requested will not meet this standard. Solicitations in which time or space restrictions apply shall identify a source from which written information is available.

• Direct contact solicitations, including personal and telephone appeals, shall identify: a) the solicitor and his or her relationship to the benefiting organization, b) the benefiting organization or cause, and c) the programs and activities for which funds are requested • Solicitations in conjunction with the sale of goods, services or admissions shall identify at the point of solicitation: a) the benefiting organization, b) a source from which written information is available, and c) the actual or anticipated portion of the sales or admission price to benefit the charitable organization or cause.

Fund-raising practices • Soliciting organizations shall establish and exercise controls over fund-raising activities conducted for their benefit by staff, volunteers, consultants, contractors, and controlled or affiliated entities, including commitment to writing of all fund-raising contracts and agreements • Soliciting organizations shall establish and exercise adequate controls over contributions • Soliciting organizations shall honor donor requests for confidentiality and shall not publicize the identity of donors without prior written permission. Donor requests for confidentiality include but are not limited to requests that one's name not be used, exchanged, rented or sold • Fund raising shall be conducted without excessive pressure. Excessive pressure in fund raising includes but is not limited to solicitations in the guise of invoices; harassment; intimidation or coercion, such as threats of public disclosure or economic retaliation; failure to inform recipients of unordered items that they are under no obligation to pay for or return them; and strongly emotional appeals which distort the organization's activities or beneficiaries.

Governance • Soliciting organizations shall have an adequate governing structure. Soliciting organizations shall have and operate in accordance with governing instruments (charter, articles of incorporation, bylaws, etc.) which set forth the organization's basic goals and purposes, and which define the organizational structure. The governing instruments shall define the body having final responsibility for and authority over the organization's policies and programs (including authority to amend the governing instruments), as well as any subordinate bodies to which specific responsibilities may be delegated. An organization's governing structure shall be inadequate if any policy-making decisions of the governing body (board) or committee of board members having interim policy-making authority (executive committee) are made by fewer than three persons.

• Soliciting organizations shall have an active governing body. An active governing body (board) exercises responsibility in establishing policies, retaining qualified executive leadership, and overseeing that leadership. An active board meets formally at least three times annually, with meetings evenly spaced over the course of the year, and with a majority of the members in attendance (in person or by proxy) on average. Because the public reasonably expects board members to participate personally in policy decisions, the governing body is not active, and a roster of board members may be misleading, if a majority of the board members attend no formal board meetings in person over the course of a year. If the full board meets only once annually, there shall be at least two additional, evenly spaced meetings during the year of an executive committee of board members having interim policy-making authority, with a majority of its members present in person on average.

• Soliciting organizations shall have an independent governing body. Organizations whose directly and/or indirectly compensated board members constitute more than one-fifth (20 percent) of the total voting membership of the board or of the executive committee will not meet this standard. (The ordained clergy of a publicly soliciting church, who serve as members of the church's policy-making governing body, are excepted from this 20 percent limitation, although they may be salaried by or receive support or sustenance from the church.) Organizations engaged in transactions in which board members have material conflicting interests resulting from any relationship or business affiliation will not meet this standard.

GOVERNMENT REGULATION

Federal. The most far-reaching federal law regulating fund-raising activities in modern America was the Tax Reform Act of 1969. It not only altered the tax consequences of charitable giving, but also had major impact on American foundations. By the mid-1970's, however, pressure was mounting for the enactment of additional federal legislation to govern charities. Purpose: to improve public accountability and curb abuses. By 1977, several bills had been introduced in Congress. The provisions of each differed, but in general their intent was to force charities to: 1) disclose how much of the money they receive goes to expenses and channel a certain percentage to their exempt charitable purposes; and 2) issue annual financial reports. One bill proposed that all charitable organizations — including churches — be subject to the stringent rules that govern private foundations. Another bill took aim at charities that solicit contributions by mail. (It was to be administered by the Postal Service and carried a formidable penalty for violators: stoppage of all mail service!)

As of this writing, no federal legislation governing fund-raising activity nationwide has been enacted in the United States (other than that involving tax benefits received by donors who give to qualifying organizations). There are several legitimate reasons why Congress has not enacted such legislation, including these.

- Although some individual donors may be unwise and even wasteful in their giving, some bureaucrats are also unwise and wasteful in their administrative duties.

- Federal controls, however well-intentioned, would inevitably erode the independence of charities, negatively affecting their ability to be innovative and creative.

- There is no evidence to suggest that government supervision necessarily leads to better decisions or to greater honesty or to sounder management (indeed, some would argue that there is evidence to suggest quite the opposite).

- There is reason to worry that federal government regulation of fund raising might lead to official bias against some charities whose causes run counter to those advocated by the administration in power, creating a kind of ''enemies list.''

- Few bureaucrats are likely to have a satisfactory understanding of the problems and opportunities confronting charities; consequently, they may act insensitively, inappropriately, or without proper concern for timing.

- Any federal effort to regulate fund-raising activity will cost money — money that, inevitably, must come from the taxpayers.

- Regulation of fund raising is a matter best reserved for the states.

If and when federal legislation governing fund raising is enacted, many fund-raising professionals expect it to have the following features.

- Provide for full disclosure, so that charities will, in fact, be accountable to the public. A requirement to report only fund-raising costs is not sufficient. If the public is to evaluate the work of a given charity, it must have information about many aspects of its operation.

- Protect the interests of the public as well as charities.

- Avoid overkill. In trying to catch a crook, we sometimes endanger the well-being and effectiveness of law-abiding citizens.

- Have nationwide applicability, so that if you are in compliance in one state, you are in compliance in all states. Otherwise, individual state registration and compliance requirements will inflict severe administrative and economic hardships on charitable organizations.

State. By 1982, a total of 35 states had passed laws regulating charitable solicitation, and legislation was pending in other states. This legislation had two origins: 1) the sensational, widely publicized disclosures of fund-raising abuses by certain "charities" in the mid and late 70's; and 2) the cumulative weight of abuses — sensational and otherwise — that had been piling up for many years.

You must, of course, make every effort to comply with state solicitation statutes. Understand, however, that it may not be easy. The difficulty is not with the statutes proper — they are not that demanding — but with two disturbing circumstances.

- Most states lack the staff necessary to interpret their statutes properly and to enforce them. This not only gives dishonest fund raisers an advantage, it also makes it difficult for you to get answers to questions you may have about a given statute or to receive other kinds of compliance help from the state agency involved.

- State statutes vary widely and sometimes wildly in their requirements. This means, for example, that if you are a college fund raiser appealing by direct mail to alumni across the country, you may be in compliance in some states and breaking the law in others.

It is possible, however, to make some summary-type statements about the various statutes. Even if the statutes change, it will be helpful for you to have an awareness-level understanding of their general intent and of the mechanics involved.

- The regulatory agency with which you must deal is usually the office of the attorney general or the secretary of state (Arkansas, Georgia, Illinois, Kansas, Kentucky, Maine, Maryland, Massachusetts, Michigan, Minnesota, Nebraska, Nevada, New Hampshire, North Dakota, Ohio, Oregon, South Carolina, Tennessee, and West Virginia). In some states, however, the regulatory agency is the division or department of licensing or business regulation (District of Columbia, Florida, Hawaii, Rhode Island, Washington, and Wisconsin). California requires that you register with its Department of Justice; and North Carolina, with its Department of Human Resources. Four states — Connecticut, Indiana, South Dakota, and Virginia — handle registration through departments of consumer affairs or consumer protection, and four other states — New Jersey, New York, Oklahoma, and Pennsylvania — handle registration through offices expressly established for that purpose (typically called "office of charities registration").

- Most of the states require registration rather than licensing, and all but three of them require that you submit some kind of annual report disclosing your charity's financial condition.

- The states vary widely on rules governing actual solicitation. The most common requirement, however, is that solicitors must produce an "authorization to solicit" statement — obtained from the appropriate state office — on request. One state (Michigan) requires solicitors to write their "license or registration number on solicitation materials," and several other states require solicitors to disclose, on request, the percentage of contributed funds that will actually go to the charity.

- Prior to 1984, many of the states had set ceilings for fund-raising costs and had stipulated that fund raisers could not exceed those ceilings. In June of that year, however, the Supreme Court ruled that state-imposed fund-raising cost limitations were unconstitutional. In a 5-to-4 decision, the Court rejected a Maryland criminal statute prohibiting solicitation by charities whose fund-raising costs exceeded 25 percent of the money raised. "There is no necessary connection between fraud and high solicitation and administrative costs," the court said. Although the ruling did not automatically signal an end to all state statutes regulating fund-raising costs, it did cause many state legislatures to pull back funding for their administration and enforcement.

For additional information about state statutes, contact the American Association of Fund-Raising Counsel (25 West 43rd Street, New York, N.Y. 10036; phone 212-354-5799). Your local Better Business Bureau may also help.

City. Many cities, especially the larger ones, have laws regulating charitable solicitation. Begin with the city licensing department and go from there.

INDEX

(Illustrations and tables are indicated by bold-faced page numbers.)